T0315053

CHIA-HUEI WU

EMPLOYEE PROACTIVITY IN ORGANIZATIONS

An Attachment Perspective

BRISTOL
UNIVERSITY
PRESS

First published in Great Britain in 2019 by

Bristol University Press
University of Bristol
1-9 Old Park Hill
Bristol
BS2 8BB
UK
t: +44 (0)117 954 5940
www.bristoluniversitypress.co.uk

North America office:
Bristol University Press
c/o The University of Chicago Press
1427 East 60th Street
Chicago, IL 60637, USA
t: +1 773 702 7700
f: +1 773 702 9756
sales@press.uchicago.edu
www.press.uchicago.edu

British Library Cataloguing in Publication Data
A catalogue record for this book is available from the British Library.

Library of Congress Cataloging-in-Publication Data
A catalog record for this book has been requested.

ISBN 978-1-5292-0057-7 (hardback)
ISBN 978-1-5292-0060-7 (ePub)
ISBN 978-1-5292-0061-4 (Mobi)
ISBN 978-1-5292-0059-1 (ePDF)

Cover design by blu inc, Bristol
Front cover: Studio Firma
Printed and bound in Great Britain by CPI Group (UK) Ltd, Croydon, CR0 4YY
Bristol University Press uses environmentally responsible print partners

Contents

List of tables and figures		v
Notes on the author		vi
Preface		vii
one	Employee Proactivity	1
	Conceptualizations of proactivity	3
	Motivational mechanisms underpinning proactivity	8
	Relational basis of proactivity: a perspective from attachment theory	12
	Overview of chapters	19
two	Introduction to Attachment Theory: Behavioural System and Individual Differences	23
	Behavioural systems	24
	Attachment behavioural system and attachment styles	32
	Internal working models	36
	Summary	42
three	Introduction to Attachment Theory: Social Contexts and Changeability	43
	Attachment style in different social contexts	44
	Stability and changeability of attachment style	47
	Summary	54
four	A Behavioural System Model of Proactivity	55
	Employee proactivity as a form of exploration	55
	A behavioural system of proactivity	58
	The link between attachment security and the behavioural system of proactivity	63
	Summary	65

five	Individual Differences in and Situational Impact on Employee Proactivity	67
	Individual differences in proactivity	67
	Situational impact on proactivity	71
	Summary	81
six	Implications for Employee Proactivity Research	83
	Relational basis of employee proactivity	84
	Dispositional foundation of proactivity	86
	Integration of different conceptualizations and motivational mechanisms of proactivity	90
	Future research on employee proactivity	91
	Application of attachment theory to work behaviour	99
	Coda	103
References		105
Index		129

List of tables and figures

Tables

2.1   Characteristics of six behavioural systems   31

4.1   Similarity between exploration and proactive   58
       behaviour

5.1   Correlations between attachment styles and   71
       proactive personality

Figures

4.1   A behavioural system of proactivity   62

4.2   Functions of attachment security on the   64
       behavioural system of proactivity

Notes on the author

Dr Chia-Huei Wu is Associate Professor at Durham University. His research in organizational behaviour focuses on proactive behaviour, personality development, work design and employees' subjective wellbeing. His work has appeared in peer-reviewed journals, including *Academy of Management Journal*, *Journal of Applied Psychology*, *Personnel Psychology*, *Journal of Management*, *Human Relations*, *Journal of Organizational Behavior*, *Journal of Occupational and Organizational Psychology* and *Journal of Vocational Behavior*, among others. He has also contributed chapters to books, including *The Oxford Handbook of Leadership and Organizations*, *The Oxford Handbook of Positive Organizational Scholarship*, *Advances in Positive Organizational Psychology*, *Advances in Global Leadership* and *Proactivity at Work*. Before joining Durham University, Dr Wu was Assistant Professor at London School of Economics from 2013 to 2018. He is an editorial board member for *Human Relations*, *Journal of Business and Psychology* and *Journal of Business Research*. He earned his PhD degree at the University of Western Australia.

Preface

What makes people more likely to initiate positive change within their organizations? I have sought to address this question during my doctoral research and adopted a relational perspective based on attachment theory to understand employee proactivity. In this book, I take the same perspective and extend my previous work by proposing a theoretical model to explain why having a sense of attachment security in social relationships can strengthen an individual's proactivity.

This book aims to bring an academic contribution from a new angle to understand why employees engage in proactive behaviour. At the same time, this project involves topicality by addressing the question of how to promote employees' proactive behaviour, which has been widely asked in management. In this book I specifically focus on how attachment theory can be used to understand motivation and antecedents of proactive behaviour but do not intend to cover all topics, such as consequences of proactive behaviour. I have made this decision because I believe a narrow focus provides a greater degree of elaboration. Another reason for focusing on motivation and antecedents of proactive behaviour is to use attachment theory to develop a theoretical framework that integrates current understandings of motivational factors in shaping proactive behaviour. Although proactivity has been widely studied, a lack of an integrative theoretical framework has resulted in a patchwork of proactivity research. In this book I seek to elaborate why attachment theory can offer a theoretical framework that integrates the existing knowledge of proactivity and indicates directions for future research.

This book is partly based on my doctoral dissertation. Here I would like to express my sincere gratitude to my doctoral supervisor, Dr Sharon Parker, who led me to study proactivity and continues to give me encouragement, guidance and support to build an academic career. I am deeply indebted to Dr Yi-Cheng Lin and Dr Kaiping Yao for their supervision during my undergraduate and postgraduate training in psychology at National Taiwan University. Dr Lin evoked my research interests in attachment theory and guided me towards studying adult attachment in several projects. Dr Yao strengthened my research interests by encouraging me to use attachment theory for a course assignment as a lens to understand religion and quality of life. It is their guidance and encouragement that have supported my research journey on attachment from the very beginning. Finally, words cannot be expressed to convey gratitude to my wife, Ya-Huei Lin, my son and daughter, Guan-Yi Wu and Hsuan-Yi Wu, for their affectionate help and support during the writing of this book.

Chia-Huei Wu
September 2018

ONE

Employee Proactivity

In today's global economy, organizations must operate within complex environments that require rapid responses to changing external circumstances (Campbell, 2000). To succeed within these increasingly uncertain operating environments, in addition to adapting to changes, employees can proactively respond to challenges (Griffin et al, 2007) to improve the work environment or facilitate personal development.

For example, to respond to anticipated challenges and industry trends, employees can create, introduce and apply new ideas at work (for example, Kanter, 1988; Scott and Bruce, 1994; Janssen, 2000). Employees also can make constructive suggestions to improve the work environment (for example, LePine and Van Dyne, 1998; Ashford et al, 2009) when identifying problems or opportunities that may influence performance of their work units or organizations. In addition, when serving customers, employees can proactively provide their service by, for example, sharing information with customers, anticipating needs that customers might have and preparing solutions in advance (Rank et al, 2007). In terms of career trajectories, individuals can be proactive at different stages to improve their employment prospects. For example, starting from job search, individuals can proactively approach potential employers, prepare different job application and interview materials for different employers, or use available networks to maximize opportunities (Blau, 1994). As newcomers, individuals can actively build relationships with colleagues, seek information and feedback from supervisors about how to perform tasks well, or negotiate job content to fully utilize their skills and interests (Ashford and Black, 1996). When performing tasks, employees can actively seek feedback from supervisors or peers to learn whether they are on the right track and regulate their behaviour and performance accordingly (Ashford et al, 2016). They also can take the initiative in shaping their careers by consulting seniors and actively building relationships with experts in specific areas (Claes and Ruiz-Quintanilla, 1998). These are just some examples of how employees can be proactive in different situation to master the work environment and facilitate their career/personal development.

As we would expect, different forms of proactive behaviour have been found to produce individual and collective benefits, such as enhanced career and work success (for example, Fuller and Marler, 2009) and improved organizational effectiveness (for example, Raub and Liao, 2012), suggesting the desirability of employee proactivity. Against this background, scholars have paid much attention to the underpinning characteristics and motivational mechanisms of employee proactivity with an aim of understanding how to promote employee proactivity at work. Although a vast amount of work has been done to understand employee proactivity (Parker and Bindl, 2017), the current understanding has several limitations that prevent us from fully understanding employee proactivity. One major limitation is a lack of a relational understanding of employee proactivity, which is the main concern addressed in this book.

The aim of this chapter is twofold. First, it provides a brief review of the current approaches to understanding employee proactivity. It starts with a review of three different perspectives on conceptualizing employee proactivity and then three identified motivational mechanisms of proactivity. Second, it elaborates on the limitations of the current understanding and specifically indicates why we need a relational understanding of employee proactivity and why attachment theory (Bowlby, 1997 [1969]) can offer a theoretical framework for such understanding.

The chapter concludes by introducing the purpose of each chapter of this book.

Conceptualizations of proactivity

So far in the literature proactivity has been examined from several different perspectives, including an individual differences perspective (Bateman and Crant, 1993), a behavioural perspective (for example, Parker and Collins, 2010) and a goal process perspective (Frese and Fay, 2001; Grant and Ashford, 2008; Bindl et al, 2012). Each perspective is explored in more detail in the following section.

Individual differences perspective

The individual differences perspective of proactivity focuses on individuals' dispositional tendency to take actions to make changes and the phenomena that people can vary in degrees of such tendency. To capture the dispositional tendency, Bateman and Crant (1993) proposed the concept of proactive personality and suggested that a person high in proactive personality is the one 'who is relatively unconstrained by situational forces and who effects environmental change' (p 105). They stated that 'proactive people scan for opportunities, show initiative, take action, and persevere until they reach closure by bringing about change' (p 105). In line with this description, by interviewing a sample of proactive businesspeople, Bateman and Crant (1999) found that people high in proactive personality actually perform seven behaviours: scanning for change opportunity; setting effective, change-oriented goal; anticipating and preventing problems; doing different things or doing things differently; taking action; persevering; and achieving results. All these behaviours are aimed at bringing about positive change in the future. Empirically, two meta-analyses (Fuller and Marler, 2009; Thomas et al, 2010) have supported the importance of proactive personality as a strong dispositional predictor of various forms of proactive behaviour.

Although conceptualizing proactivity as an individual differences trait helps identify individuals who are more proactive than others, which should help employers form a proactive workforce of employees via selection, it has several limitations. First, while acknowledging individual differences in proactivity, scholars adopting this perspective do not explain why such individual differences exist. Understanding the developmental basis of proactive personality is thus needed to strengthen the foundation of using an individual differences perspective to understand employee proactivity. Second, the individual differences perspective only helps identify who is more likely to make changes but not how s/he enacts change specifically. As those high in proactive personality can vary in their goals and engage in different proactive behaviour at work for leading different changes (Wu et al, 2018), knowing who is high or low in proactive personality is not informative for distinguishing between different proactive strivings and managing an employee proactive workforce. For example, among those who have high levels proactive personality, some could be committed to the work unit and be proactive in terms of improving its effectiveness by giving constructive voice while others could be committed to their personal career and be proactive in terms of making social connections and learning new skills in order to expand their career prospects. Therefore, studies have increasingly focused on proactive behaviours within particular situations, with proactive personality being considered as a dispositional antecedent to such behaviours, which reflects a behavioural perspective of proactivity.

Behavioural perspective

Rather than focusing on a general tendency to effect change, most studies on proactivity focus directly on behaviours that aim to bring about change. Several examples were provided earlier in the chapter to indicate different proactive behaviours serving different purposes and suited to different situations. Despite the differences, scholars in this field seek to identify core elements of proactive behaviour in order to establish a broad understanding of proactive behaviour. Three common features have been identified and used to define proactive behaviour broadly: self-initiative, future-focused and change-oriented. Proactive behaviour is self-initiated, which means that it is enacted without the actor being told to and without explicit instruction. Proactive behaviour is future-focused, which means that it aims to deal with anticipated problems or opportunities in the long-term. Proactive behaviour is change-oriented, involving not just reaction to a situation, but also being prepared to change that situation in order to bring about a different outcome. Based on these three elements, proactive behaviour has been defined as self-initiated and future-oriented actions that aim to bring about change (Crant, 2000; Frese and Fay, 2001; Parker et al, 2006).

It should be noted that the term 'proactive behaviour' is typically used to refer to positive behaviour that employees use to improve a situation or their own prospects. Although employees can also proactively engage in counterproductive work behaviour to harm their work units or organizations intentionally – for example, by expressing 'hurtful, critical, or debasing opinions regarding work policies, practices, and procedures' (Maynes and Podsakoff, 2014: 91) – such negative behaviour has not been studied in proactivity literature as the underlying motivational mechanisms of such negative behaviour can be very different from those of typical and positive proactive behaviour. This book also follows this conventional perspective in defining proactive behaviour and does not aim to explain employees' active engagement in counterproductive work behaviour.

While the behavioural perspective helps understand different forms of proactive behaviour under the same umbrella, which in turn helps depict a general understanding of proactive behaviour and integrate knowledge from studying specific forms of proactive behaviour, such an approach is challenging as it is neither easy nor reasonable to put all forms of proactive behaviour into one box. In order to take the advantage of using a unifying angle to understand different forms of proactive behaviour as well as acknowledge their differences at the same time, scholars have proposed different frameworks to classify and summarize various specific proactive behaviour into a small number of categories, a compromise approach to consider commonalities and differences between different forms of proactive behaviour. For example, Parker and Collins (2010) summarized proactive behaviour into three broad goals: achieving a better fit between the person and the environment ('proactive person-environment fit behaviour', including feedback inquiry, feedback monitoring, job change negotiation and career initiative); improving the internal organizational environment ('proactive work behaviour', including taking charge, voice, innovation and problem prevention); and improving the fit of the organization with its wider environment ('proactive strategic behaviour', including strategic scanning, issue-selling credibility and issue-selling willingness). Griffin and colleagues (2007) differentiate between proactive behaviours based on the level of the organization at which individuals direct their proactive efforts. They specify the extent to which individuals engage in self-starting, defined as future-oriented behaviour relevant to their individual work situations or roles (individual task proactivity); to a team's situation or the way the team works (team member proactivity); and to their organization and/or the way the organization works (organization member proactivity).

No matter whether a generic concept of proactive behaviour or a classification framework is used, the implicit assumption behind the behavioural perspective is that we can understand different forms of proactive behaviour under the same umbrella due to their commonalities. However, this assumption is questionable because having features in common does not mean those behaviours are the same and can be understood altogether. As such, the approach suggested by the behavioural perspective of proactivity should be justified and can be justified based on attachment theory (see Chapter Four). Moreover, the behavioural perspective focuses on the behaviour only and ignores states before and after individuals perform proactive actions. Being proactive is not only about behaving but also thinking – for example, planning and reflecting. Focusing on the behaviour only risks losing opportunities to understand how individuals develop, prepare and reflect on their proactive actions. Such concern is covered by a process perspective of proactivity.

Process perspective

In an extension of the idea that proactivity is a way of behaving that can apply across multiple domains, scholars have recently conceptualized proactivity as a goal process (Frese and Fay, 2001; Grant and Ashford, 2008; Bindl et al, 2012). In other words, when an individual tries to bring about a different future via change, they engage in conscious goal-directed processes, including both goal generation and goal striving (for example, Chen and Kanfer, 2006). Goal generation involves, for example, envisioning a different future and planning to bring about a change, whereas goal striving involves concrete steps to bring about the change, as well as reflections on these actions and their consequences. This view recognizes that both goal generation and striving are necessary for bringing about change, and also acknowledges that these processes are likely to be influenced by different antecedents (Bindl et al, 2012). From this perspective, proactivity is more than observable behaviour; it is a broader process that also involves unobservable elements like envisioning, planning and reflecting.

Empirically, several studies have supported the process view of proactivity. Within the context of career self-management, Raabe and colleagues (2007) showed that goal commitment and information collection first contribute to a person's career planning, which then leads to active career self-management behaviour that helps the person eventually achieve career success. Based on two longitudinal studies using samples of graduates making the transition from college to work, De Vos and colleagues (2009) also showed that career progress goals sustain career planning, which then contributes to networking behaviours, and, one step further, leads to higher career success in the end, supporting the envisioning-planning-performing process in proactivity. In a longitudinal study with a focus on changes in four-stage activities (that is, envisioning, planning, enacting and reflecting) in proactive goal regulation over time, Bindl and colleagues (2012) reported that those four regulatory activities were distinct and that changes in these regulatory activities over time were related to an individual's affective experiences, indicating the role of emotion in shaping one's goal regulation and achieving proactive goals.

Motivational mechanisms underpinning proactivity

Building on the process perceptive of proactivity, Parker and colleagues (2010) proposed that proactive goal generation and striving will depend on three motivational forces: whether individuals feel capable of being proactive (a 'can do' pathway); whether they have some sense that they want to bring about a different future (a 'reason to' pathway); and whether they have positive affect to foster their proactive actions (an 'energized to' pathway). Each motivational pathway is explored in more detail in the following section.

'Can do' pathway

Whether individuals feel capable of being proactive is largely determined by their self-efficacy, which refers to 'people's beliefs about their capabilities to produce designated levels of performance that exercise influence over events that affect their lives' (Bandura, 1994: 71). As behaving proactively can be risky – it can damage one's reputation if the action fails or incurs disapproval from others – having higher self-efficacy will help individuals believe that they can cope with potential setbacks and perceive a higher likelihood of success by positively weighing the costs of such risky action against the benefits. Empirically, self-efficacy has been found to predict various forms of proactive behaviour such as proactive work behaviour (for example, innovation, taking charge, giving voice and problem prevention) (for example, Wu and Parker, 2017), newcomers' proactive behaviour (for example, Gruman et al, 2006) and job search behaviour (for example, Brown et al, 2006).

Other can-do elements for proactive goals proposed by Parker and colleagues (2010) include beliefs that action is feasible (for example, control appraisals) and low perceived costs of action. For example, control appraisals – 'the individuals' expectations that they will feel control over situations and particularly that they can have an impact on work outcomes' (Parker et al, 2006: 638) – are positively related to personal initiatives (Frese et al, 2007). Regarding the perceived costs, Tidwell and Sias (2005) found that the perceived social cost in information seeking in organizations has a negative impact on overt information-seeking behaviour among newcomers. Similarly, Dutton and colleagues (1997) also indicated that context factors related to fear of negative consequences can impede willingness for issue selling. Nevertheless, in contrast to the role of self-efficacy in proactive behavior, these two aspects rarely feature in research.

'Reason to' pathway

'Even if people are certain they can do a task, they may have no compelling reason to do it' (Eccles and Wigfield, 2002: 112). Drawing on self-determination theory that emphasizes the role of intrinsic motivation in driving self-regulation process, Parker and colleagues (2010) argued that internalized or autonomous, rather than controlled, forms of motivation are the key for driving proactivity. This proposition has been supported by studies focusing on autonomous motivation directly (Wu and Parker, 2017) or factors that in common convey an intrinsic force to engaging in proactive behavior, such as motives, desires, commitment, felt responsibility for change or role perception.

For example, pro-social motives or the desire to protect and promote the wellbeing of others can drive employees to take initiative at work (Grant and Mayer, 2009). Newcomers with a higher desire for control tend to behave proactively in seeking information, networking and negotiating job change in order to master their new environment (Ashford and Black, 1996). In terms of commitment, Belschak and Den Hartog (2010; see also Den Hartog and Belschak, 2007) reported that different foci of commitment (career, supervisor, team and organization) were positively related to personal initiative and proactive behaviour at the personal, interpersonal and organizational level. Felt responsibility for change, an individual's belief that he or she is personally obligated to bring about environmental change, has been repeatedly positively linked with proactive behaviours such as taking charge (Morrison and Phelps, 1999) and change-oriented behaviour (Choi, 2007). Finally, employees are also motivated to be proactive if being proactive is perceived to be part of their work role. For example, employees with a flexible role orientation (that is, perceived breadth of experienced responsibility within the work environment) are more likely to take initiatives at work (Parker et al, 1997). Employees who perceive giving constructive voice as being part of work role make more suggestions reported by their supervisors (for example, Duan et al, 2017).

'Energized to' pathway

As proactive behaviour is self-initiated and not part of job requirements, employees need to put extra energy into doing so while fulfilling their job duties. Employees need to have energy in order to be proactive as it takes time and effort to monitor the environment, identify threats or opportunities, come up with ideas or solutions to make changes, and overcome obstacles or resistance to making things happen. In other words, from goal envisioning to goal striving, employees need to put energy into thinking and acting to initiate change. This energizing process is evident in studies concerning the role of positive affect or felt recovery in proactive behaviour.

Parker and colleagues (2010) suggest that positive affect can energize one's proactivity at both goal-envisioning and goal-striving stages. For goal envisioning, positive affect is likely to influence the selection of proactive goals because it expands thinking and results in more flexible cognitive processes (Fredrickson, 1998, 2001; Isen, 1999), which in turn helps individuals think ahead and rise to the challenge of pursuing proactive goals. In terms of goal striving, positive affect helps individuals build positive attitudes and can be more resilient when encountering obstacles in goal achievement and facilitates engagement and persistence in activities (Tsai et al, 2007). Moreover, because proactivity is self-initiated and represents internalized rather than externalized goals (Ryan and Deci, 2000), there is more scope for internal influences, such as affect. Positive affective experience has been found to help increase individuals' tendency to choose generative behaviours (Seo et al, 2004). A positive association between positive affect and proactive behaviour has been widely reported at a between-individual level such that those experiencing more positive affect tend to engage in more proactive behaviour (for example, Madjar et al, 2002; Ashforth et al, 2007; Den Hartog and Belschak, 2007). A positive association between positive affect and proactive behaviour has also been observed at a within-individual level such that individuals who experience more positive affect during a day or week tend to engage in more proactive behaviour on the same day or week (for example, Fritz and Sonnentag, 2009; Madrid et al, 2014; Wang et al, 2018).

The contribution of positive affect to proactive behaviour can also be seen in research on work engagement, which is defined as feelings of work-related vigour, dedication, and absorption (Schaufeli et al, 2002). Several studies have reported a positive relationship between work engagement and personal initiative (Hakanen et al, 2008; Salanova and Schaufeli, 2008) or self-initiative and pursuit of learning at the day level (Sonnentag, 2003). Moreover, studies on felt recovery also demonstrate an energizing process in facilitating proactive behaviour. As recovery 'reverses the negative consequences of job demands and brings an individual back to his or her pre-stressor level of functioning' (Binnewies et al, 2009: 69), employees who are highly recovered will have more energy to do subsequent work or perform proactively. In support of this, Sonnentag (2003) found that the feeling of being recovered from work in the morning predicted personal initiative and pursuit of learning on the same day (see also Binnewies et al, 2009, 2010). Altogether, there is good evidence of the beneficial role of positive affect and affect-related concepts, such as feeling recovered and invigorated, for proactive behaviour.

Relational basis of proactivity: a perspective from attachment theory

As discussed in the previous section, in order to understand how to promote employee proactivity at work, scholars have paid much attention to identifying core elements of proactive behaviour and seeking to understand core antecedents and processes and that facilitate proactivity across multiple domains. For example, proactive personality has been proposed as a core dispositional foundation of several forms of proactivity. In terms of processes, Parker and colleagues (2010) identify a set of motivational processes ('can do', 'reason to' and 'energized to') that apply to many forms of proactivity. Although such research has provided a generic understanding of employee proactive behaviour, the work so far mainly focuses on individuals as the agents who can determine and regulate their proactive thinking and actions. This focus, however, ignores the role of others in shaping one's proactivity, or a relational basis of proactivity.

Being proactive is not simply about whether an individual is inclined to master and change the environment, but also about how an individual thinks about and interacts with others. In brief, proactivity involves different aspects of relational and social consideration. First, relational experiences can shape an individual's proactive tendency in general. As individuals start to learn the contingency between their actions and responses from others, their external environment in early life (Bowlby, 1997 [1969]), and their proactive tendency or proactive personality can actually be developed from their social interaction with their primary caregivers. Second, relational experiences in an individual's current work environment can influence their proactive motivation and thus actions. For example, in order to successfully make changes, an individual may need to develop social networks to obtain the latitude and resources to achieve a proactive goal (Thompson, 2005). Moreover, proactive behaviour that aims to bring about change has been described as psychologically risky because of the discomfort this behaviour can cause in others (Parker et al, 2010), and because of the potential for damage to an individual's reputation and image if the proactivity is unsuccessful (Morrison and Bies, 1991; Ashford et al, 2003). Individuals who get along easily with others, therefore, are more likely to gather support and resources from surrounding others to facilitate their proactivity by enhancing a sense of competence and controllability (the 'can do' process), strengthening the motivation to do so (the 'reason to' process) and replenishing energy to overcome obstacles (the 'energized to' process). Moreover, individuals with different styles and schemas in interacting with others may respond differently to their current social environment at work and thus express different levels of proactivity at work. For example, Wu and Parker (2017) reported that having support from leaders is more important for motivating proactive behaviour in those who are anxious or avoidant in their social relationships at work than those who are not. This finding suggests that the impact of relational experiences in shaping proactive behaviour at work can be complex if we consider the interaction effects between individuals' relational styles and social characteristics of the work environment. These relational impacts, however, have not been properly examined.

The aim of this book is to offer a theoretical framework to unpack relational basis proactivity based on attachment theory (Bowlby, 1997 [1969]). Attachment theory is a well-known concept that explains how the relationship between children and their primary caregivers in early life influences children's social–psychological development. However, attachment theory is more than a theory for understanding child behaviour and development. It provides an explanation for why human beings engage in certain behaviours, how personality is shaped from early relational experiences, and how personality continues to influence and is influenced by life experiences and behaviour in the later life, concepts that are introduced in Chapters Two and Three. Because of these features, as elaborated in Chapters Four and Five, attachment theory provides a theoretical framework for conceptualizing proactive behaviour, understanding the development of proactivity and motivational mechanisms in triggering proactive behavior, and depicting individual differences in such development. Moreover, as attachment theory emphasizes the role of relational experiences in human development, it explains how relational experiences can shape individuals' proactive behaviour, offering a theoretical framework to underpin the relational basis of proactivity. For example, it provides a theoretical justification for understanding different forms of proactive behaviour under a broader concept, underpinning the three motivational mechanisms from a relational perspective and explaining why people vary in their proactive tendencies. It also offers propositions for unpacking the interaction effects between individuals' relational styles and the current social environment in shaping proactive behaviours. Overall, the book suggests that attachment theory can bring new insights to understanding proactive behaviour and advancing our studies on employees' proactivity, which is further discussed in Chapter Six.

But why adopt attachment theory in particular, given that the role of early experiences in shaping personality development has been examined in many personality theories, especially theories rooted in the traditional psychoanalytic paradigm (see Westen et al, 2008, for a review)? This section provides reasons why attachment theory is a better one to help us understand human behaviour than other theories rooted in the traditional psychoanalytic paradigm.

In fact, attachment theory is influenced by traditional psychoanalytic paradigm. Based on the reflection of both the psychoanalytic approach and clinical experiences in observing maternal deprivation and separation, Bowlby (1997 [1969]) proposed attachment theory to explain affective responses and behaviours of institutionalized children who were separated from their parents. These reflections and clinical experiences mean that attachment theory takes a very different approach compared with the traditional psychoanalytic approach in explaining human behaviour and personality development. However, attachment theory also shares some ideas with the psychoanalytic paradigm. Against this background, the following section briefly outlines the features of attachment theory that are similar to and different from the psychoanalytic paradigm to provide a broader background of attachment theory. This brief illustration provides answers for why attachment theory was adopted to understand proactive behaviour.

First, in line with the perspective of the traditional psychoanalytic paradigm (see Westen et al, 2008, for a review) that early life experiences are important in shaping one's personality and behaviour in later life, Bowlby (1997 [1969]) proposed that early interactions with primary caregivers determine one's personality. However, in contrast to the traditional psychoanalytic paradigm's retrospective approach of constructing earlier life experiences in clinical interviews and linking patients' syndromes to them, Bowlby (1997 [1969]) focused on observations of child behaviour and experiences in real-life situations, and then used these observations to examine how early life experiences in childhood influence personality development. In other words, Bowlby (1997 [1969]) adopted a prospective approach to understanding personality development that provided a rigorous basis for testing the role of early experiences in shaping personality development. Moreover, attachment theory provides concepts that can be operationalized and hypotheses that can be tested. It not only theorizes how important early life experiences can be, but also provides testable concepts and hypotheses to examine how early life experiences can influence one's personality development and behaviour in later life. This is also the reason why attachment theory, more often than traditional psychoanalytic theories, has been used to guide empirical studies in various areas of psychology.

Second, attachment theory provides more precise concepts and contexts for understanding how early life experiences can shape personality development. For example, in line with object relations theories (theories evolved from traditional psychoanalytic paradigm; see Westen et al, 2008, for a review) that stress the importance of the mental representations of the self and others that are developed from general interpersonal relationships, attachment theory suggests that the relationship between a child and primary caregiver is the most important interpersonal context for developing mental representations (that is, the 'internal working model') of self and others. In other words, object relations theories do not specify which interpersonal relationships are important for shaping mental representations of self and others, or who the 'significant others' are, whereas attachment theory suggests that the interpersonal relationship between the child and the primary caregiver is the key relationship context. Moreover, in contrast to rather imprecise arguments for the formation of mental representations and generic descriptions of mental representations (such as good or bad) in object relations theories, attachment theory indicates specific factors that influence the development of internal working models, such as caregivers' sensitivity and responsiveness, and proposes specific dimensions of the self concepts or other concepts that result from attachment interactions, such as worthiness of being loved and trust in others (Kirkpatrick, 1995).

Third, as opposed to the traditional psychoanalytic paradigm, attachment theory incorporates an ethological and evolutionary element to understand the motivation of human beings, which therefore provides ethological functions of human behaviour and also different views on the structure and process of personality development. For example, Bowlby (1997 [1969]) proposed that human infants, like infants of other species, rely on older and mature adults to feed and protect them from predators or other dangers. Thus, in order to achieve evolutionary adaptiveness (survival and reproduction), attachment behaviours, such as crying and seeking the protection of an attachment figure that can provide support and care, are adaptive responses for humans as well as other species. In this model, behaviour is not governed by 'drives' with a drive-reduction process, as suggested in the traditional psychoanalytic paradigm, but the goal of the behaviour with a goal-corrected control process. That is, the presence of certain behaviours is governed by a behavioural system that activates or deactivates to deal with demands in a given situation. Although several behavioural systems that could govern different types of behaviour to achieve evolutionary adaptiveness have been identified, Bowlby (1997 [1969]) proposed that the attachment behavioural system is the central system that shapes the operation of other systems to serve the end goals of survival and reproduction. This system therefore underpins the structure of personality by specifying several behavioural systems that govern the process of personality. As such, attachment theory provides a clear theoretical framework for understanding why relational dispositions can shape proactive behaviour. That is, the attachment behavioural system plays a key role in shaping the operations of other behavioural systems, including the behavioural system governing proactive behaviour.

In sum, attachment theory addresses some of the disadvantages of the traditional psychoanalytic paradigm by proposing new approaches to understand personality development. It revises the methodological approach, improves cognitive roles with the concept of the internal working model, replaces a drive-reduction motivational model with a control system model, and provides a framework for understanding the structure and process of personality development. However, because along with the traditional psychoanalytic paradigm it aims to understand the role of early life experiences in personality development, attachment theory has been considered a new version of personality theory (for example, Cervone and Pervin, 2008; Westen et al, 2008). As such, attachment theory offers a better theoretical framework than traditional psychoanalytic theories to unpack the role of relational dispositions in shaping human behaviour.

Overview of chapters

To provide an overview of this book, this section outlines the purpose of each chapter.

The aim of Chapters Two and Three is to introduce attachment theory to provide a knowledge background for applying the theory to understand employee proactivity. Chapter Two introduces the concept of behavioural system in attachment theory and then specifically elaborates the development and operation of an attachment behavioural system, the central behavioural system that can shape operation of other behavioural systems. The chapter elaborates how the development of the attachment behavioural system shapes individuals' internal working models of self, others, and the broader social environment that continue to guide an individual's attitudes, beliefs and behaviours in later life.

Chapter Three discusses context-specific attachment styles and the stability and changeability of attachment styles. An attachment relationship exists not only between children and parents, but also in other relationship contexts. Context-specific attachment relationships, such as attachment at work, are more proximal to influencing behaviour in the specific contexts. This theoretical proposition helps illustrate how relationships in organizations are important in shaping employee proactivity. Attachment theory also suggests the changeability of attachment style as individuals' prototype of attachment style and internal working models of self, others and the broader social environment can change when they encounter different experiences. This proposition addresses the issue of psychosocial development and suggests opportunities for personal interventions.

Chapters Four and Five apply attachment theory to understand proactive behaviour. Chapter Four builds a behavioural system model of proactivity based on attachment theory and elaborates the role of attachment security in shaping the operation of the behavioural system. The chapter first indicates that proactive behaviour, as a form to challenge the status quo, can be conceptualized as a form of exploration in which instigators aim to master their environment through self-directed change efforts. Next, building on the idea of exploration behavioural system from attachment theory, the chapter specifically offers a behavioural system of proactivity. As a behavioural system is operated in a goal-corrected manner, in which individuals regulates their behaviour and goals in a feedback loop, the behavioural system of proactivity incorporates the process perspective of proactivity and the three identified motivational mechanisms of employee proactivity reviewed in the current chapter. Finally, Chapter Four elaborates how attachment security can influence the operation of the behavioural system of proactivity, building a relational foundation for proactivity.

Next, Chapter Five looks into individual and situational factors of attachment security to offer a relational perspective to explain why there are individual differences in employee proactivity and how managers and organizations can influence employee proactivity. The chapter first discusses how we can use the concept of attachment styles to explain individual differences in employee proactivity. It then elaborates how an employees' relationships with different targets at work (for example, relationships with supervisors, work groups, and organizations) can influence their sense of attachment security at work and shape their proactivity at work.

Chapter Six highlights the implications for employee proactivity research of the proposed model and propositions outlined in Chapters Four and Five. First, it discusses how attachment theory provides a different angle from alternative approaches for understanding the relational basis of employee proactivity. It then elaborates how attachment theory strengthens a dispositional approach to understanding employee proactivity and outlines the value of the proposed model in integrating different conceptualizations and motivational mechanisms in proactivity research. Finally, the chapter indicates avenues for future research on employee proactivity specifically and elaborates how attachment theory can help us understand work behaviour broadly.

TWO

Introduction to Attachment Theory: Behavioural System and Individual Differences

The aim of this chapter is to introduce three aspects of attachment theory (Bowlby, 1997 [1969]): the concept of behavioural systems, which Bowlby (1997 [1969]) proposes to explain behaviours; how the attachment behavioural system is developed from early interaction experiences with primary caregivers; and how the development of the attachment behavioural system shapes individuals' internal working models of self, others and the broader social environment that continue to guide an individual's attitudes, beliefs and behaviours in later life.

The chapter first reviews the concept of the behavioural system – the core concept of attachment theory. Bowlby (1997 [1969]) proposed this construct to explain how instinctive behaviours are governed by specific set goals for achieving evolutionary adaptiveness. This concept is the key to understanding proactive behaviour as this book conceptualizes proactive behaviour as a form of exploration behaviour governed by the exploration behavioural system with the goal of mastering the environment to serve the end goal for survival and reproduction, and then relies on this conceptualization to theorize how attachment styles can shape proactive behaviour.

The chapter then reviews the development and operation of the attachment behavioural system – the core behavioural system whose operation is shaped by the interaction experiences between infants and their primary caregivers. This section elaborates on individual differences in the operation of the attachment behavioural system (that is, attachment styles) that are due to the different earlier interaction experiences. The idea of individual differences in attachment styles is important to the understanding of proactivity because it helps explain how the different operations of the attachment behavioural system shape different operations of the exploration behavioural system, and thus helps explain proactive behaviour.

Finally, the chapter introduces the concept of the internal working model – a cognitive representation of oneself and the external social environment. It describes how an internal working model is developed from early interaction experiences and consolidated over time, and then becomes a part of personality, reflecting individuals' beliefs, attitudes and expectations in social relationships (see Collins and Read, 1994; Collins and Allard, 2002). Because individuals have different interaction experiences with their primary caregivers, the contents of their internal working models are also different, and these in turn are related to the attachment styles they develop. This discussion of the formation of internal working models and the individual differences among them is important for understanding proactivity because it explains the underlying motivational mechanisms behind attachment styles and proactive behaviour.

Behavioural systems

Bowlby (1997 [1969]) proposed the concept of behavioural systems to explain the presence or absence of instinctive behaviours. Rather than treating instinctive behaviour as a stereotyped movement of species, Bowlby (1997 [1969]: 39) suggested that instinctive behaviour is 'an idiosyncratic performance by a particular individual in a particular environment—yet a performance that nonetheless follows some recognizable pattern and that in a majority of cases leads to some predictable results of benefit to individual or species'. In order to explain how an idiosyncratic performance by a particular individual occurs in a particular environment, Bowlby (1997 [1969]) proposed that instinctive behaviour is mediated by a behavioural system.

A behavioural system is an inherited behavioural programme from the evolutionary selection process and serves a specific function. For example, the attachment behavioural system serves the function of protection so that mammal infants can attach to mature adults to protect them from dangers. A behavioural system has a particular 'set goal' that denotes a specified motor performance or a specified relation between the individual and environment. For example, the set goal of the attachment behavioural system is the degree of proximity to an attachment figure. Using the set goal as criterion, a behavioural system operates as a control system with a 'goal-corrected' process by taking account of the discrepancy between initial status and the effects of current performance. According to Bowlby (1997 [1969]), a behaviour system does not govern only one sort of behaviour, but a set of interchangeable and functionally equivalent behaviours for achieving the same set goal. Hence, depending on situational demands, different forms of behaviour governed by the same behavioural system will be chosen to attain a particular goal state in particular situations. For example, when infants encounter a threat, they will desire closer proximity to their attachment figures via different attachment behaviour, such as crying, touching, following and calling, depending on the degree of proximity needed.

A behavioural system is activated when bodily and mental states and the perceived environmental stimuli make the set goal of the system salient. It is terminated when a set goal is achieved. Thus, the activation and termination of a behavioural system determine the presence or absence of the governed instinctive behaviour for achieving evolutionary adaptedness (that is, survival and reproduction). The activation and termination of a behavioural system involve several cognitive appraisals, such as appraisal of internal states and perceived environmental stimuli, appraisal of the progress of current behaviour (that is, whether progress is smooth or stopped) and appraisal of following consequences of outcomes (that is, changes of external environment or internal states and achievement of a set goal).

In recognizing that there are different behavioural systems, Bowlby (1997 [1969]) proposed several ways that different behavioural systems can be coordinated in different structures. The simplest structure is chain structure, in which behavioural systems are linked sequentially. In this structure, when one behaviour is done in correct sequence, the next behaviour in the sequence will be taken. In other words, the termination of one behavioural system will lead to the activation of the next. However, this chain structure is not flexible, because if one behaviour in the chain structure fails, the whole behavioural sequence will be shut down. Thus, Bowlby (1997 [1969]) proposed that the chain structure could be more flexible by allowing each behavioural system to have more links to other behavioural systems at the same time. Therefore, if one behaviour in the chain structure fails to activate one of behavioural systems, the other behavioural systems can be activated to achieve the same outcome by using other alternative behaviours.

In addition to a chain structure, Bowlby (1997 [1969]) suggested that various behavioural systems could share the same causal factors based on Tinbergen's (1951) study on instinct behaviour. In other words, different behavioural systems can be activated by the same factor, for example when male sex hormones lead to various masculine behaviours (such as fighting and courting). In the same vein, the same environmental stimuli or internal states can also lead to various behaviours. In this way, behavioural systems are organized by casual factors in a hierarchical structure, and environmental stimuli and the individual's bodily and mental state will together determine which behaviour will be performed. A more flexible possible organization of behavioural systems is the structure of 'plan hierarchy' proposed by Miller and colleagues (1960). They suggested that the overall structure of human behaviour is goal-corrected and hierarchical, and that a primary goal can be served by the attainment of sub-goals that are constituted by yet lower-level goals. In this way, the behaviour structure becomes more flexible to adapt to various environments because a primary goal can be achieved via various alternative routes. Bowlby (1997 [1969]: 80) suggested that behavioural systems across species can also be organized in a mixed way, using chain structure, casual hierarchy and/or plan hierarchy, but 'in the higher vertebrates behavioural systems are more often environmentally liable, responsive to more complex cues and in their means of integration more likely to include causal or plan hierarchies. In man these trends have been carried a very long way further'.

In order to have better coordination among behavioural systems and achieve a set goal with efficient behaviour, an individual needs a cognitive model of the environment and a cognitive model of the self in order to draw up a plan to achieve a set goal. Bowlby (1997 [1969]) termed this cognitive model the 'internal working model'. According to Bowlby (1997 [1969]: 80), the function of the internal working model is to 'transmit, store and manipulate information that helps in making predictions' in achieving a set goal. Broadly, the model of environment includes both the physical and social environment that an individual deals with, and the model of self includes working knowledge of one's own behavioural skills, potentialities and capabilities. An internal working model is constructed based on available experiences and is applicable to potential situations. As Bowlby stated (1997 [1969]: 81), 'the more adequate the model, the more accurate its predictions; the more comprehensive the model, the greater the number of situations in which its predictions apply'. Although an internal working model is useful when it is stable to help individuals make plans to achieve set goals in different situations and predict potential consequences, it should also be kept up to date with continuous but minor modification. However, when major changes in environment or in the self occur, large changes in the internal working model are needed to help an individual adapt to the new situation. Hence, although the internal working model is relatively stable, it is also changeable and revisable.

Nevertheless, behavioural systems in human beings, although they are in place at birth, are not well developed at first. In the same way that an internal working model is developed from experiences, behavioural systems also become more sophisticated and integrated over the course of development. Bowlby (1997 [1969]) proposed that a behavioural system can exist in a simpler form in the beginning such that it can be activated by a wide range of triggers and would not need to be well coordinated or integrated in order to achieve a set goal in a plan hierarchy. However, as the individual gains experience and an increased ability to discriminate, different stimuli are increased, and triggers for that behavioural system will be restricted in order to maximize its benefit for evolutionary adaptedness within the environment. Moreover, when an individual becomes mature, simpler or independent behavioural systems will become more sophisticated and integrated with other behavioural systems to achieve a set goal in a plan hierarchy. This development is not only characterized by the goal-corrected systems developed in the course of development, but also by individuals' increasing awareness of the set goals they have adopted, by their developing increasingly sophisticated plans for achieving them, and by their increasing ability to relate one plan to another, to detect incompatibility between plans and to order them in terms of priority (Bowlby, 1997 [1969]:153).

Finally, it should be noted that there are various behavioural systems with varying degrees of complexity. Bowlby (1997 [1969]) did not aim to identify all behavioural systems. Rather, he suggested that the attachment behavioural system is the most crucial behavioural system developed in infancy since it determines an individual's personality characteristics and has enduring influence in later life. However, his behavioural system approach can be extended to understand other kinds of human behaviour that can be regarded as instinct behaviour designed to maximize evolutionary adaptedness. For example, Bowlby (1997 [1969]) and other researchers (for example, Mikulincer and Shaver, 2003, 2012; Cassidy, 2008) have identified a few other behavioural systems. These behavioural systems include caregiving, exploration, affiliation, sexual and power behavioural systems. As mentioned previously, each behavioural system is designed from natural selection to serve a specific function for evolutionary adaptedness (that is, survival and reproduction) and the function is governed by the set goals of that system. To provide a clearer illustration, the following section discusses these behavioural systems in terms of their biological functions and how these functions operate, summarized in Table 2.1.

First, in terms of biological function, the attachment behavioural system is aimed at protecting the individual from danger with the set goal of maintaining proximity to attachment figures (Bowlby, 1997 [1969]); the caregiving behavioural system is aimed at increasing the survival and reproduction of those who have shared genes with the set goal of providing support and care for others (Bowlby, 1997 [1969]; Mikulincer and Shaver, 2012); the exploration behavioural system is aimed at mastering the environment for survival with the set goal of acquiring knowledge of the environment (Bowlby, 1997 [1969]; Cassidy, 2008); the affiliation behavioural system is aimed at increasing efficiency in learning, ability in living, and accessibility of a mate, with the set goal of being sociable with others (Cassidy, 2008); the sexual behavioural system is aimed at reproducing genes in the next generation with the set goal of having sexual intercourse with opposite-sex others (Mikulincer and Shaver, 2003, 2012); and the power behavioural system is aimed at acquiring and controlling resources for survival and reproduction with the set goal of removing threats and obstacles that interfere with a sense of control (Mikulincer and Shaver, 2012).

As mentioned previously, these behavioural systems are only activated when needed and thus they are activated by different triggers. Specifically, the attachment behavioural system is activated when the individual detects physical threats or psychological separation of attachment figures (Bowlby, 1997 [1969]); the caregiving behavioural system is activated when an individual detects another's need for help in confronting danger or stress or pursuing challenging goals (Mikulincer and Shaver, 2012); the exploration behavioural system is activated when the environment is complex and or when conflict, novelty or uncertainty require efforts to acquire knowledge to understand and master the environment (White, 1959; Berlyne, 1960; Loewenstein, 1994); the affiliation behavioural system is activated when an individual sees that others can contribute to the individual's own wellbeing, help respond to a challenge or defend against a threat (Weiss, 1998); the sexual behavioural system is activated when an individual notices an attractive and sexually interested partner (Mikulincer and Shaver, 2012); and the power behavioural system is activated when an individual finds that others are trying to acquire the individual's valued resources or constrain the individual's access to such resources (Shaver et al, 2011). Nevertheless, behavioural systems are not automatically activated when their corresponding triggers are detected. Rather, as mentioned previously, the activation and termination of a behavioural system involve several cognitive appraisals, and cognitive models of the environment and the self (that is, the internal working model) guide the overall set goal and the plan of performed behaviour at a particular time.

Based on the concept of behavioural systems, this book conceptualizes proactive behaviour as a type of exploration behaviour governed by the exploration behavioural system, and relies on this conceptualization to understand how attachment

Table 2.1: Characteristics of six behavioural systems

Behavioural systems	Biological function	Set goal	Triggers
Attachment behavioural system	Protect individual from danger	Maintain proximity to attachment figures	Physical threats or psychological separation of attachment figures
Caregiving behavioural system	Increase the survival and reproduction of those who have shared genes	Provide support and care for others	Others' needs for help in confronting danger or stress or pursuing challenging goals
Exploration behavioural system	Master the environment for survival	Acquire knowledge of the environment	Complex, conflict, novelty or uncertainty in the environment
Affiliation behavioural system	Increase efficiency in learning, ability in living, and accessibility of mate	Be sociable with others	Others who can contribute to one's wellbeing or help respond to a challenge or defend against a threat
Sexual behavioural system	Reproduce genes in the next generation	Have sexual intercourse with opposite-sex others	Attractive and sexually interested partner
Power behavioural system	Acquire and control resources for survival	Remove threats and obstacles that interfere with a sense of control	Others who are trying to acquire valued resources or constrain access to resources

styles shape proactivity (see Chapter Four). In sum, in attachment theory, Bowlby (1997 [1969]) proposed the behavioural system approach to understand human instinct behaviour. Although several behavioural systems have been identified, Bowlby (1997 [1969]) has suggested that the attachment behavioural system is the crucial system for personality development. This suggestion is reviewed in the next section.

Attachment behavioural system and attachment styles

This section specifically examines the attachment behavioural system because it is the central behavioural system in human development and influences the development of other behavioural systems according to attachment theory.

Based on attachment theory, the attachment behavioural system is designed to protect infants from danger with the set goal of maintaining proximity to attachment figures. It is activated when potential internal or external threats or distress are present and when separation from the attachment figure is detected. This behavioural system develops in the first year and continues to mature and to influence an individual's proximity-seeking strategy and behaviour in later life. At different development stages, different types of behaviour for seeking proximity are used. For example, in the earlier stages, crying and smiling are apparently attachment behaviours infants use to attract an attachment figure's attention and maintain proximity. But later, when infants can move by crawling, they can follow the attachment figure to maintain proximity. As the individual matures from childhood to adulthood, the need to maintain proximity with the attachment figure will gradually depend less on the physical presence of the attachment figure and physical contact with the attachment figure, and more on cognitive strategies such as confidence in the attachment figure's ability to provide protection, memory of the attachment figure's caregiving behaviour and related experiences in the past, and activation of security-based self-representations developed from past interaction with attachment figures (Mikulincer and Shaver, 2007a). Thus, according to Bowlby (1997 [1969]), the attachment behavioural system governs a repertoire of behaviours, and an individual can choose one or more that are evaluated as most appropriate in a particular situation to meet the set goal of proximity maintenance.

Because the attachment behavioural system is developed from and shaped by the interaction experiences between the infant and primary caregiver, different patterns of attachment occur in infants with different interaction experiences with their primary caregivers. It should be noted that caregivers' and infants' characteristics together shape the pattern of attachment of an infant. For example, infants vary in the degree to which they demand attachment. Moreover, different infants may provide different feedback to responses from their caregivers. Some infants, for example, may smile more than others when they are content. These differences in infants will influence the parental behaviour of their primary caregivers. Moreover, primary caregivers' attitude, ability and skill in dealing with infants' needs may also vary. Some caregivers, for example, may have lower tolerance for noise and hence respond impatiently to crying. Hence, attachment, as an interactive relationship between an individual and a primary caregiver, is determined by both infants' and caregivers' characteristics.

Nevertheless, Bowlby (1997 [1969]) indicated that different histories of parental response will result in different attachment styles. Specifically, sensitivity and responsiveness to infants' needs and readiness for social interaction are two main characteristics that may result in an infant who demonstrates secure attachment, while lack of such sensitive responding may result in insecure attachment. The first empirical study about different attachment styles was conducted by Ainsworth and colleagues (1978). They assessed the attachment between mothers and children and classified infants as having secure, avoidant or ambivalent attachments by categorizing behaviours in the 'strange situation', a series of separation and reunion episodes. Ainsworth and colleagues (1978) found that secure attachment is fostered when an infant experiences consistent caregiver warmth and availability. On the other hand, avoidant attachment is fostered through caregiving that is characterized by unavailability or insensitivity, and ambivalent attachment is developed through inconsistent or intrusive caregiving.

These three patterns of attachment can be regarded as strategies in the operation of the attachment behavioural system (Main, 1990; Mikulincer and Shaver, 2003) and thus the reason for infants' different patterns of attachment is that they adopt different strategies in operationalizing their attachment behavioural system. According to Main (1990) and Mikulincer and Shaver (2003), secure attachment reflects the primary strategy of the attachment behavioural system; that is, infants tend to seek and maintain proximity to their primary caregivers when they detect potential internal or external threats or distress, or separation from the attachment figure. However, when primary caregivers are unavailable and unresponsive, the aforementioned primary strategy in the operationalizing attachment behavioural system cannot be applied in practice and thus infants will adopt secondary strategies to deal with the distress by either hyperactivating or deactivating the attachment behavioural system.

The hyperactivating strategy is to intensify the desire of proximity in order to obtain caregivers' support and care. This strategy is more likely to be adopted by infants whose caregivers sometimes give proper feedback and sometimes do not, because their caregivers still can provide appropriate care, and if infants can provide stronger signals, their caregivers are more likely to notice their needs and response to them (Main, 1990). In contrast, the deactivating strategy is to reduce the desire for proximity in order to avoid the distress of the unavailability the attachment figure and even prevent potential harm caused by attachment requests. This strategy is more likely to be adopted by infants whose caregivers always provide improper feedback or reject requests to be attached because the infant's request for attachment may have negative consequences, such as being alienated or rebuffed by their caregiver (Main, 1981; Cassidy and Kobak, 1988). Over time, these different strategies in operationalizing the attachment behavioural system become more enduring and begin to constitute a part of one's personality, which is referred to 'attachment style'.

According to the recent development of attachment-style assessment, the three attachment styles (that is, secure attachment, avoidant attachment and ambivalent attachment) can be represented in a two-dimensional framework with the dimensions of attachment anxiety and attachment avoidance (Brennan et al, 1998). Attachment anxiety represents the extent to which an individual is anxious or fearful about abandonment or being unloved, whereas attachment avoidance represents the extent to which an individual is uncomfortable with closeness and dependence on others. In this two-dimensional framework, those who are securely attached in a traditional, secure attachment category are those who have lower scores on both attachment anxiety and attachment avoidance. Those who are avoidantly attached in the traditional avoidant attachment category are those who have higher scores on attachment avoidance but low on attachment anxiety. Those who are ambivalently attached in the traditional ambivalent attachment category are those who have higher scores on attachment anxiety but lower scores on attachment avoidance. Those having higher scores on both dimensions are individuals who have unstructured or disorganized attachment styles, in Ainsworth and colleagues' (1978) report. The four quadrants also consistently map on to the four attachment categories proposed by Bartholomew and Horowitz (1991). This two-dimensional framework has been widely used in adult attachment literature and these dimensions have been linked to perceptions of the self, such as self-esteem and self-concept clarity (for example, Lopez et al, 2002; Wei and Ku, 2007; Wu, 2009); perceptions of social relationships, such as social support and relationship satisfaction (Mallinckrodt and Wei, 2005; Tsagarakis et al, 2007; Wu and Yao, 2008); interpersonal behaviours at work, such as citizenship and helping (Geller and Bamberger, 2009; Richards and Schat, 2011); exploration willingness (Green and Campbell, 2000); and psychological wellbeing (Wei and Ku, 2007; Wu and Yao, 2008).

Attachment experiences not only shape the operation of the attachment behavioural system, but also influence the formation of mental representations towards environment and self. The next section reviews theoretical propositions and empirical findings related to internal working models developed from attachment experiences.

Internal working models

This section introduces the concept of internal working models and reviews studies examining its functions in shaping one's beliefs, attitudes and behaviours. Such an understanding helps understand the underling mechanisms behind the association between attachment styles and proactive behaviour that is elaborated in Chapter Four.

As mentioned previously, in order to achieve a set goal, an individual needs cognitive maps of the environment or the self to create a plan of action and predict potential consequences. In attachment relationships, the associated mental representations are internal working models of how the physical world may be expected to behave, how an individual's mother and other significant persons may be expected to behave, how the individual may be expected to behave and how each interacts with the others. Within the framework of these working models, individuals evaluate their situation and make their plan. And within the framework of the working models of mother and individual, individuals evaluate special aspects of their situation and make their attachment plans (Bowlby, 1997 [1969]: 354).

Given that an individual receives consistent patterns of caregiving in childhood, the individual's internal working models are gradually consolidated. These internal working models will become an important part of personality and will reflect the individual's beliefs, attitudes and expectations in social relationships. The stability of internal working model is summarized by Bowlby as follows:

> Whatever representational models of attachment figures and of self an individual builds during his childhood and adolescence, tend to persist relatively unchanged into and throughout adult life. As a result, he tends to assimilate any new person with whom he may form a bond, such as a spouse or child, or employer or therapist, to an existing model (either of one or other parent or of self), and often to continue to do so despite repeated evidence that the model is inappropriate. Similarly, he expects to be perceived and treated by them in ways that would be appropriate to his self-model, and to continue with such expectations despite contrary evidence. (1979: 142)

Internal working models have been found to be related to one's memories of social relationship and beliefs, attitudes and expectations about self, others and relationships (see Collins and Read, 1994; Collins and Allard, 2002). Because individuals have different attachment experiences, the contents of these internal working models are also different. First, internal working models are developed from attachment experiences; thus, internal working models reflect attachment-related memories. Several studies have shown that adults with different attachment styles represent their attachment experiences differently. For example, in a retrospective report, Hazan and Shaver (1987) found that adults with secure attachment are more likely than adults with insecure attachment to describe their relationships with parents as being affectionate, caring and happy; their mother as being respectful, confident, accepting, responsible, not intrusive and not demanding; and their father as being caring, loving, humorous and affectionate. Adults with anxious attachment are more likely than adults with avoidance attachment to describe their mother as being humorous, likable, respected and not rejecting, and their father as being unfair. Similar findings were also obtained by Feeney and Noller (1990) with the same retrospective approach, such that securely attached adults described their early family relationships as positive, avoidantly attached adults reported more childhood separation experiences with their mother, and anxiously attached adults described their father as less supportive. The same pattern was also found in cognitive tasks. When participants were asked to recall attachment-related memories, securely attached adults were faster to retrieve positive attachment-related memories, whereas insecurely attached adults were faster to retrieve negative attachment-related memories (for example, Mikulincer and Orbach, 1995; Mikulincer, 1998). More recently, Dykas and Cassidy (2011) reviewed empirical findings in childhood, adolescence and adulthood and found that securely attached individuals are open to both positive and negative attachment-related experiences and memories and tend to construct positive attachment-related memories, whereas insecure attached individuals tend to suppress attachment-related memories or recall them negatively.

Second, internal working models influence attachment-related beliefs, attitudes and expectations about self, others and relationships. In secure attachment, caregivers always give feedback in effective ways and at proper times, which makes securely attached individuals form a belief that they are worthy of being loved, which then helps them develop a positive self-concept. In contrast, without sensitive and responsive feedback, insecurely attached individuals tend to form a belief that they are not lovable and hence develop negative self-concepts. Many studies have supported this argument by showing that securely attached individuals have higher self-esteem and possess stronger positive self-views than insecurely attached individuals, especially people with anxiety attachment styles (for example, Hazan and Shaver, 1987; Collins and Read, 1990; Bartholomew and Horowitz, 1991; Mikulincer, 1995; Roberts et al, 1996; Brennan and Bosson, 1998; Park et al, 2004; Wu, 2009). Moreover, because secure attachment experiences provide stable and reliable social interactions, securely attached individuals also tend to form a clear and well-organized self-concept compared with insecurely attached individuals for whom no social interaction can be relied on to help them understand who they are. In line with this idea, several studies have found that securely attached individuals have higher self-perception accuracy (Kobak and Sceery, 1988; Dozier and Lee, 1995; Berger, 2001), self-concept clarity (Wu, 2009), and integrated and coherent self-concept structure (Mikulincer, 1995).

In terms of the concept of others, securely attached individuals tend to develop feelings of trust and dependence toward their caregivers, and belief that if they need it they can gain support from caregivers. Accordingly, securely attached individuals tend to possess a model of others as responsive and trustworthy. In contrast, insecurely attached individuals tend to possess a negative model of others as unreliable and untrustworthy (especially for people with avoidance attachment styles). For example, Hazan and Shaver (1987) reported that securely attached individuals are more likely than insecurely attached individuals to think that other people are generally well-intentioned and good-hearted. Collins and Read (1990) also reported that securely attached individuals tend to view others as trustworthy, dependable and altruistic; anxiously attached individuals tend to view others as complex and difficult to understand; and avoidantly attached individuals tend to view others as untrustworthy and unreliable, and are more likely to doubt the honesty and integrity of others.

Internal working models also shape individuals' expectations of their relationships. Using 'if-then' propositions as a research method, in their first study, Baldwin and colleagues (1993) asked participants to consider several hypothetical attachment-relevant scenarios (for example, 'If I depend on my partner') and then to rate the likelihood of positive and negative outcomes in the interaction (for example, 's/he accepts you' or 's/he rejects you'). In the second study, they used a lexical decision task to ask participants to judge whether a target stimulus is a 'word' or 'non-word' after presenting a hypothetical attachment-relevant or attachment-irrelevant scenario. The target stimuli include words for positive and negative outcomes (for example, support or leave) and other non-words as control. In both studies, results showed that securely attached individuals have more positive if-then expectancies than insecurely attached individuals. In the first study, securely attached individuals perceived a higher likelihood of positive outcomes in different hypothetical scenarios and insecurely attached individuals perceived a higher likelihood of negative outcomes in different hypothetical scenarios. In the second study, securely attached individuals were faster to recognize words for positive outcomes, whereas avoidantly attached individuals were faster to recognize words for negative outcomes, especially when the hypothetical scenarios were related to interpersonal trust. These findings suggest that the internal working models of people with different attachment styles contain different ways of viewing themselves, others and relationships.

More importantly, because a function of internal working models is planning and organizing behaviour to achieve attachment security (Bowlby, 1997 [1969]), internal working models are also related to the specific goals and strategies in social interaction (Collins and Read, 1994; Collins and Allard, 2002). Securely attached individuals are more likely to seek a balance between closeness and autonomy depending on the presence or absence of dangers. For example, they are more likely to seek proximity to attachment figures and social support when facing stressful life events (Ognibene and Collins, 1998; Mikulincer et al, 2002) but are more likely to engage in exploration activities when no distress is present (Mikulincer, 1997; Green and Campbell, 2000). Anxiously attached individuals are more likely to seek high levels of intimacy to fulfill their need for approval, and they alleviate their fear of rejection with excessive reassurance seeking (Shaver et al, 2005) and tend to use emotion-focused strategies in coping with stressful events (Mikulincer and Florian, 1995). Avoidantly attached individuals are more likely to seek high levels of autonomy to avoid potential harm in social interactions. They are likely to focus on non-attachment-related goals such as personal achievement (Brennan and Morris, 1997; Hepper and Carnelley, 2010) and tend to use distancing coping strategies when facing stress events (Mikulincer and Florian, 1995).

In a more intensive study examining the role of internal working models, Collins (1996) asked participants to describe how they would interpret, emotionally react and behaviourally respond to negative attachment-relevant events (for example, 'your partner didn't respond when you tried to cuddle'). Her findings revealed that securely attached individuals tended to interpret the hypothetical events as more positive, compared with insecurely attached individuals. Securely attached participants also had less emotional distress towards the events and adopted behaviours that would be less likely lead to conflict in the relationship. Anxiously attached individuals tended to negatively interpret the events, had strong emotional distress and adopted behaviours that would be more likely to bring conflict in the relationship. Finally, avoidantly attached individuals also tended to negatively interpret the events and adopt conflict behaviour, but in contrast to anxiously attached individuals, they did not feel strong emotional distress towards the events.

In sum, the current findings show that internal working models play a role in influencing cognitive, emotional and behaviour responses in social relationships (Collins and Read, 1994).

Summary

This chapter has reviewed core ideas in attachment theory by introducing the concept of behavioural systems, how the attachment behavioural system is developed and how the development of the attachment behavioural system shapes individuals' internal working models. The focus so far mainly concerns the interaction between individuals and their caregivers. Nevertheless, attachment theory also suggests that an individual can develop different attachment relationships with different targets, which can influence the stability or changeability of attachment styles. The next chapter reviews attachment theory and literature regarding attachment relationships in different social contexts, and stability and changeability of attachment style.

THREE

Introduction to Attachment Theory: Social Contexts and Changeability

The aim of this chapter is to introduce attachment theory (Bowlby, 1997 [1969]) in terms of context-specific attachment styles, and the stability and changeability of attachment style.

An attachment relationship exists not only between children and parents, but also in other relationship contexts. Bowlby (1997 [1969]) has suggested that when people cannot build a securely attached relationship with their primary caregivers, they will try to find secondary attachment figures. Moreover, when individuals grow up, their life domain is not restricted to their family, parents or primary caregivers. An individual's attachment behaviour may be directed to persons, groups or institutions other than the family, and these targets can serve as subordinate attachment figures or principal attachment figures for some people. This proposition suggests that a context-specific attachment relationship is more proximal to influencing behaviour in that specific context, which provides the necessary background for understanding attachment relationships at work when discussing employees' proactive behaviour.

This issue also implies the changeability of attachment style. Although attachment style and the internal working models developed from early life experiences are relatively stable and constitute one's personal characteristics, attachment theory also posits that people's attachment style and internal working models can be changed when they encounter different experiences. This proposition addresses the issue of psychosocial development and suggests opportunities for personal interventions.

Attachment style in different social contexts

Although attachment theory suggests that an individual's attachment style is primarily shaped by interaction experiences with primary caregivers, it also suggests that an individual can have different attachment relationships with different persons and thus form different attachment styles across different contexts. Specifically, Bowlby stated:

> During adolescence and adult life a measure of attachment behavior is commonly directed not only towards persons outside the family but also towards groups and institutions other than the family. A school or college, a work group, a religious group or a political group can come to constitute for many people a subordinate attachment-'figure,' and for some people a principal attachment-'figure.' (1997 [1969]: 207)

Several empirical studies have supported this view by examining attachment to family, friends and partners (Overall et al, 2003; Sibley and Overall, 2008), attachment to supervisors (Game, 2008), attachment at work (Neustadt et al, 2006), attachment toward social groups (Smith et al, 1999) and attachment to God (Granqvist and Kirkpatrick, 2008). This extension suggests that context-specific attachment experiences will also shape individuals' behaviour, and it has been found that current context-specific attachment experiences have a stronger effect in shaping one's attitude and behaviour in that context (for example, Smith et al, 1999; Cozzarelli et al, 2000; Bennett et al, 2008).

In the literature, the relationship between context-specific attachment styles and the prototype attachment style has been theorized in different ways. First, based on the idea of assimilation, the prototype attachment style governs the development of context-specific attachment styles because individuals tend to rely on their existing relational schema to expect and interpret a new social relationship. Supporting this perspective, Feeney and colleagues (2008), in an adolescent sample, reported that attachment styles can predict behaviours (that is, support-seeking and support-giving behaviours) in interactions with strangers, suggesting that the formation of new social relationships is influenced by the prototype attachment styles. Relevant to this, Overall and colleagues (2003) provide further evidence to show that attachment to family, friends and partners is influenced by a common latent factor representing the prototype attachment style.

However, based on Baldwin and colleagues' (1996) idea, the prototype attachment style and context-specific attachment styles can be different relational schemas in an individual's social-cognitive representation network. Accordingly, prototype attachment style and context-specific attachment styles can have their own impact in shaping an individual's attitudes, beliefs and behaviours. Supporting this view, Pierce and Lydon (2001) first reported that context-specific relational models and the global relational model are related but distinct constructs. They also found that context-specific relational models will be generalized to the global relational model over time and that global models will then shape specific models over time, implying reciprocal dynamics between context-specific and prototype attachment styles. In their second study (Pierce and Lydon, 2001), these authors further reported that both global and specific relational models can explain individuals' interaction experience. Similarly, Game (2008) found that both prototype attachment style and supervisor-specific attachment can predict emotional response in different hypothetical relationship event scenarios.

Nevertheless, several studies have shown that the global and specific relational models have their impacts on different outcomes, instead of the same outcome, suggesting that the global and specific relational models operate in different ways. First, Cozzarelli and colleagues (2000) demonstrated that the global relational model had a stronger impact on overall psychological adjustment, whereas the specific relational models had a stronger impact on the relationship-specific outcomes (for example, feelings of romantic love or relationship satisfaction), revealing that global and specific relational models operated at different levels. Bennett and colleagues (2008) found that supervisor-specific attachment can predict supervisory alliance and supervisory style variables, but the prototype attachment style cannot. These findings suggest that context-specific attachment experiences shape one's attitude and behaviour in that context. Smith and colleagues (1999) provided stronger evidence by showing that only group-specific attachment style can predict group-related constructs (for example, collective self-esteem), whereas romantic attachment style cannot, revealing that context-specific attachment styles have differential impacts across contexts.

In summary, attachment theory and related empirical findings have supported the idea that an individual can possess not only a prototype attachment style developed from earlier interaction experiences, but also different context-specific attachment styles based on interaction experiences with different targets. Based on the current findings that the prototype attachment style and context-specific attachment styles can shape each other and can have different impacts on an individual's attitudes, beliefs and behaviours, the whole attachment system is thus revealed to be more complex and dynamic. This suggests that in addition to the prototype attachment style, context-specific attachment styles should also be taken into account when attitudes, beliefs, and behaviours in specific contexts are investigated. Such examination is theoretically important as Bowlby (1997 [1969]) has suggested that when individuals cannot build a securely attached relationship with their primary caregivers, they will try to find secondary attachment figures. According to this compensation hypothesis (Granqvist and Kirkpatrick, 2008), it is important to examine whether positive relational experiences in other relationship contexts will bring more benefit to those who are low in attachment security. Having different attachment experiences within different relationship contexts also suggests the possibility of attachment changes, especially when different social interaction experiences are encountered (Bowlby, 1997 [1969]). The next section specifically reviews the issue of the stability and changeability of attachment styles.

Stability and changeability of attachment style

Although the attachment style developed from earlier interactions with primary caregivers tends to be stable over time and to become an enduring personal characteristic (Fraley, 2002; Fraley et al, 2011), it is also changeable, especially when an individual encounter changes in the maternal environment (for example, Vaughn et al, 1979; Egeland and Farber, 1984) or specific life events or experiences (for example, Hammond and Fletcher, 1991; Kirkpatrick and Hazan, 1994; Ruvolo et al, 2001; Simpson et al, 2003). Similar to the ideas of assimilation and accommodation proposed by Piaget (1953), Bowlby (1997 [1969]) suggests that when the current experiences cannot be explained and assimilated by the existing schema of attachment relationships (that is, internal working models), individuals will tend to update their existing schema to accommodate the new experiences. Thus, changes in the social environment or specific life events or experiences, which render new experiences, are more likely to results in changes in attachment style and the associated internal working models. Hence, Mikulincer and Shaver (2007a: 118) summarized that 'attachment patterns are rooted in both early interactions with primary caregivers and later attachment experiences that challenge the validity of the early working models'.

Past results have shown that attachment style has moderate stability over years, revealing that an attachment style is relatively stable but still open to change. For example, Fraley's (2002) meta-analysis of 27 longitudinal studies covering a timespan from infancy to early adulthood found that stability of attachment styles (secure versus. insecure) is moderate ($r = .39$). Mikulincer and Shaver (2007a: 141) summarized 36 longitudinal studies about stability of attachment styles in adulthood, ranging from one week to 25 years. They found that the averaged test-retest correlations of continuous score of attachment styles is 0.56 and the averaged test-retest concordances of classifications of attachment styles is 70% (that is, 70% participants are in the same classifications of attachment styles over time). Therefore, the longitudinal findings showed moderate stability of attachment styles, and suggested that attachment style is relatively stable but still open to change.

Based on the idea that attachment style is dynamically shaped over time by both early experiences and current experiences, the important issue about the stability and changeability of attachment style is not to argue whether attachment style can be changed or not, but to figure out when an individual will change attachment style. According to the existing literature, this issue can be addressed by two approaches. The first approach is use longitudinal studies to identify how environmental change or specific life events can lead to the change of attachment style, and the second approach is to use experimental manipulations to understand whether one's attachment style can be shaped in a short time. The remainder of this section reviews studies that use these two approaches respectively.

First, several studies have indicated that one's attachment style can be changed when different or new life experiences are encountered that influence the availability, sensitivity and responsiveness of caregivers or attachment figures. For example, studies on attachment in childhood have revealed that children become insecure from 12 to 18 months of age when their mother experiences more stress and reduces the quality of caregiving and vice versa (for example, Vaughn et al, 1979; Egeland and Farber, 1984). Similarly, in a study examining stability and change of attachment at 14, 24, and 58 months of age, Bar-Haim et al (2000) showed that mothers who have children whose attachment styles changed from secure to insecure during the research time reported more negative life events and less positive life events than mothers whose children maintained a secure attachment style. Two studies focusing on stability and change of attachment at 12 and 18 months of age also showed that children were more likely to become insecure when their mothers suffered substance abuse, lower levels of relationship satisfaction or more negative life events (Vondra et al, 1999; Edwards et al, 2004). These findings suggest that changes of maternal environment can change an individual's attachment style.

More studies have focused on how specific life events or experiences can lead to the change of attachment style. These studies overall reveal that life events that change the availability of attachment figures will have more impact on the attachment style. For example, change of sleeping arrangement, loss of a parent, parental divorce, life-threatening illness of parent or child (for example, heart attack, cancer), parental psychiatric disorder, or physical or sexual abuse by a family member will lead an individual to become more insecure from infanthood to early adulthood (for example, Lewis et al, 2000; Waters et al, 2000; Sagi-Schwartz and Aviezer, 2005). Several studies have also found that romantic relationship difficulty, unsupportive romantic relationships or breakups will lead an individual to become more insecure (for example, Hammond and Fletcher, 1991; Kirkpatrick and Hazan, 1994; Ruvolo et al, 2001). Such life events or experiences can lead individuals to become more insecure partly because the availability, sensitivity and responsiveness of attachment figures are decreased during these events. In contrast, life events or experiences implying an increase in the availability, sensitivity and responsiveness of attachment figures can lead individuals to become more secure. For example, initiating new romantic relationships, marriage or positive interpersonal experiences (such as a partner's attention, love and acceptance) can lead an individual to become more secure (for example, Kirkpatrick and Hazan, 1994; Davila et al, 1999; Crowell et al, 2002; Davila and Sargent, 2003).

However, some studies have not found the expected results for the relationship between studied life events and changes of attachment styles (for example, Scharfe and Bartholomew, 1994; Davila et al, 1997; Cozzarelli et al, 2003; Davila and Cobb, 2003). One reason for this could be that subjective appraisals and feelings are more important than objective events for altering one's attachment style, because different individuals may have different interpretations and coping strategies to deal with the same life events, especially in their associated cognitive representations (Davila and Sargent, 2003; Simpson et al, 2003). Another reason to explain the inconsistent findings about life events and changes of attachment style is that some individuals do not develop a clear attachment strategy or prototype and tend to have large fluctuations in their attachment assessment because of higher vulnerability. These people are classified by Ainsworth and colleagues (1978) as having disorganized attachment. Several studies have found that this individual differences explanation provides a better prediction of changes in attachment style than the life events explanation (for example, Davila et al, 1997; Cozzarelli et al, 2003; Davila and Cobb, 2003). Thus, when examining the association between life events and changes of attachment style, the impact of individual differences should be taken into account.

Second, several experimental studies have demonstrated that priming participants with attachment-related stimuli subliminally or supraliminally (that is, security priming) can temporarily shape their attachment orientation in line with the manipulation (Mikulincer and Shaver, 2007a; Gillath, et al, 2008). The idea behind this approach is in line with the spreading activation theory of memory (Collins and Loftus, 1975; Anderson, 1983) that stimuli associated with a sense of security can create a spreading activation process to induce the associated response pattern. This approach is warranted, because an individual can have different interaction experiences with different people (Bowlby, 1997 [1969]) and thus can possess different relational schemas corresponding to a range of attachment orientations. Accordingly, because different relational schemas are available for an individual to process social interaction experiences, Baldwin and colleagues (1996) suggested that the relative accessibility of these relational schemas becomes important for determining an individual's attachment style. For example, people who are securely attached have and maintain greater access to a positive and supportive relational schema than insecurely attached people. However, this perspective also suggests that attachment styles can change when the accessibility of different relational schemas changes. For example, strengthening the accessibility of security-related relational schemas can heighten an individual's sense of security.

In line with this perspective, several studies have attempted to examine whether exposing participants to security-attachment related experiences can increase one's sense of security and induce corresponding responses in the laboratory. Several methods have been used to activate a sense of security in the laboratory, including priming with security-related words such as love, hug, affection and support (for example, Mikulincer and Shaver, 2001, Study 1) or the names or visualization of attachment figures who can provide support (for example, Baldwin et al, 1996; Baldwin and Meunier, 1999; Mikulincer and Shaver, 2001, Study 3; Mikulincer et al, 2001, Study 4; Carnelley and Rowe, 2007); priming with pictures representing attachment security (Mikulincer et al, 2001, Studies 1-3); and asking participants to recall memories of being loved and supported by attachment figures (for example, Mikulincer and Shaver, 2001, Study 1), or asking people to imagine such scenarios (for example, Mikulincer and Shaver, 2001, Study 2; Carnelley and Rowe, 2007). These experimental techniques have been found to create short-term changes in participants' sense of security in the laboratory and to lead participants to process information or behave in ways that are consistent with the activated secure attachment style, such as attenuating negative reactions to out-groups, having a positive attitude towards unfamiliar and novel stimuli, and soothing stress-related responses in threatening contexts (Mikulincer et al, 2001, 2006; Mikulincer and Shaver, 2001).

Given that security priming can promote one's sense of security in the laboratory, some research has attempted to investigate whether the benefits of security priming can be maintained over a longer period. Supporting this notion, two studies have reported long-term effects of security priming. Carnelley and Rowe (2007) used a repeated security-priming paradigm to examine whether repeated security priming can change participants' views of themselves and their relationships, or their attachment style. At Time 1, participants completed measures of relationship expectations, self-liking, self-competence and attachment styles in two dimensions (that is, attachment anxiety and avoidance). At Time 2, one week later, participants in the experimental group were asked to write descriptions for ten minutes about a person with whom they felt secure. At Time 3, one day later, each participant in the experimental group was asked to write about an experience of being supported by others in a problematic situation for ten minutes. At Time 4, participants in the experimental group were again asked to write descriptions for ten minutes about the person with whom they felt secure. From Time 2 to Time 4, participants in the control group were asked to write for ten minutes about one neutral event. Finally, at Time 5, two days later, the same measures used in Time 1 were assessed again. The results showed that participants who received repeated security priming increased their positive relationship expectation and self-views and decreased their attachment anxiety from Time 1 to Time 5, but participants who received neutral priming did not.

In another study, Gillath and Shaver (2007, as cited in Gillath et al, 2008) asked participants to complete measures of self-esteem, mood, compassion and creativity at Time 1. Unlike Carnelley and Rowe (2007), they extended dependent variables to affective response (that is, mood) and functions of caregiving behavioural systems (compassion) and exploration behavioural systems (creativity) because these constructs had been theorized as being related to attachment security (Bowlby, 1997 [1969]) and empirically supported in past studies (Green and Campbell, 2000; Mikulincer et al, 2001, 2005). Participants were then assigned to either a security-priming group or a neutral-priming group, and completed priming sections for the following three weeks (three weekdays per week). All participants were asked to complete cognitive tasks for each priming session, but participants in the security prime condition were exposed subliminally to security-related words (such as secure, embrace and love) and participants in the neutral prime condition were primed with neutral words (such as funnel and lamp). Participants completed these same measures again at the end of the priming period (Time 2) and one week after (Time 3). By analyzing data at Time 1 and Time 3, the researchers found that participants in the experimental condition had higher self-esteem, positive mood and compassion toward others than participants in the control group at Time 3, but that there was no difference at Time 1. A similar but not significant pattern was also found on creativity. Thus, these two studies showed that repeated security priming can have a lasting effect beyond the end of the priming procedure.

In sum, both longitudinal, correlational studies and experimental studies have revealed that an individual's attachment style is open to change. This change is tied to the salience of encountered experiences, such as new experiences that cannot be explained by an individual's existing relational schema or experiences that evoke different relational schema with high accessibility in the current or in a given time period. Thus, changes in attachment styles can be chronic or momentary depending on the degree of the impact of encountered experiences.

As indicated by Bowlby (1997 [1969]) and elaborated by Baldwin and colleagues (1996), individuals will have different interaction experiences with different people throughout life, and it is likely that they will develop context-specific attachment styles and associated relational schemas for different social contexts. The context-specific relational experiences may be influenced by the attachment style prototype developed from the early interaction experiences in an assimilation process; however, the context-specific relational experiences can also reshape the prototype of attachment styles in an accommodation process (Pierce and Lydon, 2001).

Summary

This chapter has reviewed core ideas in attachment theory in terms of the role of context-specific attachment styles, and the stability and changeability of attachment style. Based on this and the previous chapter, attachment theory provides a theoretical basis for explaining individuals' attitudes, beliefs and behaviours via the development of attachment styles from social interaction experiences in a general or specific context. The next chapter examines how to apply attachment theory to understand proactivity.

FOUR

A Behavioural System Model of Proactivity

The aim of this chapter is to build a behavioural system model of proactivity based on attachment theory. Drawing on key propositions reviewed in Chapter Two, this chapter develops a behavioural system model of employee proactivity in two steps.

The next section adopts a behavioural perspective (see Chapter One) and elaborates why we can conceptualize proactive behaviour as a form of exploration. In brief, proactive behaviour, as a form to challenge the status quo, can be conceptualized as a form of exploration in which instigators aim to master their environment through self-directed change efforts. The following section, pp 58–62 uses the idea of the exploration behavioural system from attachment theory (see Chapter Two) to understand proactive behaviour and specifically to propose a behavioural system of proactivity. As a behavioural system is operated in a goal-corrected manner, in which individuals regulates their behaviour and goals in a feedback loop, the behavioural system of proactivity incorporates the process perspective of proactivity and helps integrate the identified motivational mechanisms of employee proactivity (see Chapter One).

Employee proactivity as a form of exploration

The meaning of exploration is rather unspecific in the original language of attachment theory, in part because the focus was on operationalizing exploration (as a child's investigation of new and unfamiliar environments) rather than outlining a detailed conceptual discussion. However Elliot and Reis's (2003) analysis of the exploration concept identified that exploration is closely tied to effectance motivation (White, 1959; Ainsworth, 1990), defined as 'the desire for effective, competent interactions with the environment and … as an innate, organismic propensity that impels the individual to investigate, manipulate, and master the environment' (Elliot and Reis, 2003: 318). Exploration can also be externally elicited by such stimuli as novelty and uncertainty (Berlyne, 1960) or violation of expectations (Hebb, 1955; Hunt, 1963; Piaget, 1969). Whether stimulated internally or externally, according to Loewenstein's (1994) information-gap perspective, exploration involves seeking information to reduce the knowledge gap between what one knows and what one wants to know. Exploration can thus be understood as behaviour aiming to master one's environment effectively by reducing knowledge gaps, especially in the face of novelty, complexity and uncertainty.

Proactive behaviour can be seen as a form of adult exploration. For example, when behaving proactively, individuals 'take charge' of their work environments to bring about change (Morrison and Phelps, 1999), they actively solicit feedback instead of waiting to receive it (Ashford et al, 2003), and they seek out mentors and build networks to sculpt their careers (Ashford and Black, 1996). Defining features of these proactive behaviours include the fact that they are self-initiated rather than directed by others, involve bringing about change and taking control of situations rather than adapting to them, and are future-oriented and anticipatory rather than purely reactive (Parker et al, 2010). Proactivity, like exploration, stems from the desire to actively control one's environment (Bateman and Crant, 1993).

In one model of work behaviour, Griffin and colleagues (2007) argued that proactivity is most important in uncertain contexts that involve variability and lack of predictability in work tasks and role requirements (Wall et al, 2002). In these contexts, managers cannot anticipate and pre-specify all expected requirements; there is a gap between which behaviours are needed and which can be identified in advance. Individuals who are proactive engage in self-initiated actions to fill the gap created by uncertainty. In other words, proactive behaviour involves exploring unfamiliar situations and possibilities. As discussed by Frese and Fay (2001), personal initiative, a concept of proactive behaviour at work, requires the individual to scan the environment actively for potentially important cues and to find a way forward that is not obvious.

As such, proactive behaviour involves exploration aimed at bringing about change and causing things to happen. In these challenging and promotive actions, individuals strive to find and use alternative ways to approach expected future outcomes. Such efforts involve effective motivation in mastering the environment and invoking a mechanism to reduce discrepancies between the current condition and the expected condition, which is similar to the way in which exploring unfamiliar situations is characterized. To summarize similarity between exploration and proactive behaviour, Table 4.1 lists the situations required for exploration and proactive behaviour, functions of exploration and proactive behavior, and motivation behind exploration and proactive behaviour.

Based on this conceptual analysis, it can therefore be suggested that proactive behaviour in a form to challenge the status quo is governed by the exploration behavioural system identified by attachment theory. The next section adapts the idea of the operation of the exploration behavioural system specifically to propose a behavioural system of proactivity.

Table 4.1: Similarity between exploration and proactive behaviour

	Exploration	Proactivity
Situation	Novelty, complexity, uncertainty and conflict (Berlyne, 1960)	Novelty, complexity, uncertainty (Griffin et al, 2007)
Function	Seeking information to reduce the knowledge gap between what one knows and what one wants to know (Loewenstein, 1994)	Actively scanning the environment for potentially important cues and finding a way that is not obvious to bring about change (Frese and Fay, 2001)
Motivation	To master the environment (White, 1959)	To manipulate and control the environment (Bateman and Crant, 1993)

A behavioural system of proactivity

Based on the concept of the behavioural system, proactive behaviour is governed by a desire to reduce a discrepancy between a goal and the current status. When individuals perceive a discrepancy between what they would like to bring about and the current status, they will take proactive action aimed at reducing the perceived gap, to make the change happen. As attachment theory does not provide detailed theorizing regarding the operation of a behavioural system, it is possible to incorporate ideas from the goal-regulation literature (for example, Carver and Scheier, 1982; Klein, 1989; Locke and Latham, 1990; Ford, 1992) and proactivity literature (for example, Frese and Fay, 2001; Parker et al, 2010) to illustrate the operation of the behavioural system clearly. Figure 4.1 presents a schematic model for this purpose.

The operation of the behavioural system starts from a goal-envisioning process in which an individual identifies a proactive goal, or the change they would like to bring about. The proactive goal then produces a discrepancy between the status the individual wants to achieve and the current status, which triggers the operation of the behavioural system to reduce such discrepancy by planning and perforating actions towards achieving the goal. After performing a proactive behaviour, the individual will evaluate the effectiveness of such performance to see if the performed behaviour has moved the situation towards the desired status. Such a discrepancy-reduction loop will operate continually until the proactive goal is achieved. It should be noted that the operation of the behavioural system involves both a proactive discrepancy production and a reactive discrepancy reduction (Bandura and Locke, 2003) such that an individual first sets a goal to challenge the status quo that creates discrepancy and then strives to reduce the discrepancy for achieving the goal.

Although discrepancy production and reduction are key to driving the operation of the behavioural system, perceiving discrepancy itself may not always engender a proactive action. Three factors have been identified in the goal–regulation literature (for example, Klein, 1989; Locke and Latham, 1990; Ford, 1992) that can influence an individual's motivation for taking actions for goal striving: goal expectancy (that is, the likelihood of attaining the specified goal), goal importance (whether the goal is perceived by the individual to be important and attractive) and regulatory energy (whether the individual has enough energy for goal striving). In brief, individuals are more likely to take actions to make changes when they believe such change is achievable and important and when they have enough resources and energy to undertake the journey when faced with obstacles such as resistance from others.

Specifically, **goal expectancy** refers to an individual's expectation of achieving the desired goal. In expectancy theory (Vroom, 1964), expectancy refers to a belief that one's effort will result in a specific performance that will help achieve a specific outcome. Having such belief, however, is not enough, as Bandura and Locke (2003: 92) indicate 'an important difference between belief in the utility of effort and belief that one can get oneself to mobilize and sustain a required level of effort in the face of impediments, failures, setbacks, and bouts of discouragement along the way'. The concept of self-efficacy, a belief in one's capability to exercise some measure of control over one's own functioning and over environmental events (Bandura, 1971, 2001), thus captures a broader construct than effort expectancy in goal regulation and achievement. **Goal importance** refers to the perceived importance of approaching the specific goal. It captures the attractiveness of goal attainment (Klein, 1989) and influences the individual's attitude towards goal regulation in terms of the motivation and effort aimed at reducing the discrepancy (Hollenbeck and Williams, 1987). **Regulatory energy** refers to the energy required by the individual to regulate the way in which they approach a specific goal according to the circumstances. Goal regulation is an energy-consuming activity as it involves a control process that requires awareness of the environment and an ability to change behaviour accordingly in order to achieve the goal (Ford, 1992). As the level difficulty required to achieve a goal depends on the amount of effort needed to reduce the perceived discrepancy, the levels of energy necessary for tackling different goals will also vary. Previous research on goal regulation has mainly focused on factors reflecting goal expectancy and goal importance, and suggests a joint effect of goal expectancy (that is, the expectancy of attaining that goal) and goal importance (that is, the attractiveness of goal attainment) on one's commitment to tackling the goal (see Klein, 1989). As indicated by Klein (1989: 159), 'Other things being equal, individuals are more likely to remain committed to a goal when they have a high expectancy of reaching it and when their perceived value of goal attainment is high'. In addition to the joint function of goal expectancy and goal importance, Ford (1992) contends that regulatory energy should also be considered and have a joint effect with goal expectancy and goal importance in shaping motivation for goal attainment. In other words, an individual is motivated to tackle a specific goal when goal expectancy, goal importance and regulatory energy are all strong enough to facilitate goal attainment.

Having elaborated the operation of the behavioural system, this section now turns to proactive behaviours governed by the behavioural system. Following Bowlby's idea of behavioural system for human behaviour (1997 [1969]), it could be argued that the behavioural system of proactivity governs various forms of proactive behaviour and a specific form of proactive behaviour will be chosen depending on context. For example, voice (LePine and Van Dyne, 1998), innovation (Scott and Bruce, 1994) and job crafting (Wrzesniewski and Dutton, 2001) are different forms of proactive behaviour (Parker and Collins, 2010), have different natures and have been studied separately as different subjects. However, these behaviours can be regarded as different behavioural output of the behavioural system of proactivity. For example, voice can be used to make changes by offering suggestions through social influencing channels. Innovation can be used to come up with new ideas for completing tasks or improving work processes. Job crafting, a behaviour aimed at changing job content and scope to fit an individual's interests and needs, can be used when there is a disparity between an individual's job and their personal interests. These behaviours may be used individually, sequentially or simultaneously depending on the progress of goal striving. For example, when an individual fails to bring about change simply by making suggestions to others, they could consider coming up with a new idea to overcome the barrier or changing their job content and scope as a way to shift responsibility. As such, depending on the circumstances, different forms of proactive behaviours will be chosen to achieve particular goals in particular situations. This highlights the role of individual agency and consideration in the operation of the behavioural system as proactive behaviour is tailored according to the context and demands of the situation. In other words, the behavioural system is not passive and mechanistic but can be operated flexibly to respond to circumstances.

The behavioural system described here helps integrate proactivity literature in three ways. First, it incorporates a process view of proactivity (for example, Frese and Fay, 2001; Parker et al, 2010) (see Chapter One) by specifying stages from envisioning, planning, performing and reflecting. Second, it covers the 'can do', 'reason to' and 'energized to' motivational mechanisms of proactive behaviour (Parker et al, 2010) in terms of the role of goal expectancy, goal importance and regulatory energy in the goal-regulation process. Finally, it provides a theoretical basis for studying various forms of proactive behaviour under a broad umbrella.

Figure 4.1: A behavioural system of proactivity

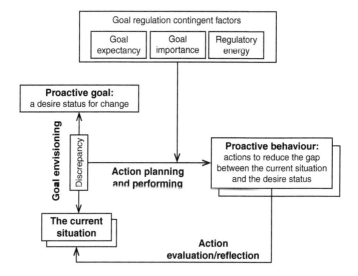

The link between attachment security and the behavioural system of proactivity

As theorized in attachment theory (see Chapter Two), attachment behavioural system is the central system that should activate behavioural systems for other purpose such as caring or exploration. In other words, attachment security should be achieved first in order to enable the operation of the behavioural system of proactivity. As the main concern of this book is to understand proactive behaviour, it does not discuss the operation of the behavioural system of attachment but rather elaborates how attachment security can facilitate the operation of the behavioural system of proactivity. Following this, the model described in Figure 4.1 can be expanded to include attachment security in order to indicate its central role in enabling the operation of the behavioural system of proactivity, as depicted in Figure 4.2.

Attachment security serves as a secure base to the operation of the behavioural system of proactivity (Bowlby, 1988), enabling an individual to explore and initiate changes. Attachment security can help an individual choose a proactive goal, because the knowledge that someone will always be there to provide support when needed gives the individual the confidence to seek, interact with and master the external environment (Grossmann et al, 2008). Based on this, it could be argued that attachment security facilitates goal envisioning, identifying goals for bringing about change.

In addition, attachment security provides self-regulatory resources with respect to positive self-view, autonomous motivation and energy, which helps strengthen goal expectancy, goal importance and regulatory energy for achieving proactive goals. Specifically, attachment theory contends that individuals perceive themselves to be worthy of love and thus have a positive self-view when cared for and supported by the attachment figure, which equates with the idea of sociometer theory that being liked and loved by others can boost one's self-esteem (Leary, 1999). Such a positive self-view in turn increases self-belief in terms of agency and capability in goal attainment, contributing to higher goal expectancy and to proactive behaviour via a 'can do' pathway.

The theory also suggests that attachment security helps individuals develop autonomous motivation (Deci and Ryan, 1985) as they are able to approach goals based on their own interests by having support from others. Strong autonomous motivation can thus help individuals focus on important goals

Figure 4.2: Functions of attachment security on the behavioural system of proactivity

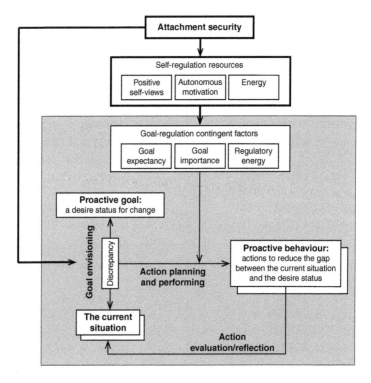

as they can determine their choice of goal, contributing to proactive behaviour via a 'reason to' pathway.

Finally, attachment security can boost energy (Luke et al, 2012), as interaction with secure attachment figures increases an individual's autonomy, relatedness and competence, which in turn boosts positive emotion and wellbeing (Deci and Ryan, 1985; Ryan and Deci, 2000) and contributes to feelings of aliveness and vivacity (Ryan and Frederick, 1997). Having higher energy can thus help an individual pursue goals whose attainment require more time and effort, reflecting an 'energized to' pathway for motivating proactive behaviour.

In brief, attachment security provides a relational basis for supporting proactivity by facilitating goal envisioning and fuelling resources to sustain goal attainment and make things happen.

Summary

This chapter has sought to propose a behavioural system model of proactivity based on the idea of attachment theory. So far it has incorporated ideas from goal-regulation literature and previous proactivity research to offer an integrative model for understanding how individuals regulates their proactive behaviour. The model also relies on attachment theory to suggest how attachment security can facilitate the operation of the behavioural system model of proactivity. The next chapter focuses on the concept of attachment security and elaborates why there are individual differences in proactivity and how managers and organizations can promote employee proactivity by developing employees' sense of attachment security in the workplace.

FIVE

Individual Differences in and Situational Impact on Employee Proactivity

This chapter aims to look into individual and situational factors of attachment security to offer a relational perspective to explain why there are individual differences in employee proactivity and how managers and organizations can influence employee proactivity. First, the concept of attachment styles is used to explain individual differences in employee proactivity. The chapter then elaborates how relationships with different targets at work (for example, relationships with supervisors/leaders, work groups and organizations) can influence employees' sense of attachment security at work and shape their proactivity at work.

Individual differences in proactivity

Why do people differ in their general propensity to be proactive? According to attachment theory, the answer lies in individual differences in the development of attachment styles from earlier interactions with caregivers. In brief, based on the proposition regarding a positive link between attachment security and proactivity, individuals displaying high levels of attachment security in their attachment styles are more likely to be proactive. As such, among the three attachment styles (that is, secure attachment, avoidant attachment and ambivalent attachment), individuals possessing secure attachment styles with their caregivers are more likely to be proactive than individuals with avoidant attachment or ambivalent attachment styles.

Individuals possessing secure attachment styles tend be proactive because, first, they are future-oriented and are able to identify goals to bring about changes that will influence their future (that is, goal envisioning) and second, they tend to possess positive self-views, have stronger autonomous motivation, and experience energy from interactions with others, and thus have more goal-regulatory resources for approaching proactive goals. They are more likely to be future-oriented because, through reliable interactions with their caregivers, they understand the relationship between their actions and the subsequent feedback. This in turn enables them to develop a sense of contingency, using their actions to influence future events. Supporting this line of reasoning, Laghi and colleagues (2009) found secure attachment to parents and peers in adolescents was positively correlated with future orientation, and noted that 'those who are secure in their attachment and in peer relationships consider themselves to be more capable and willing to explore, which is widely intended as an autonomous and proactive ability to make future plans' (2009: 191). Future orientation can contribute to individuals' proactivity because it helps individuals think ahead, identify goals that they would like to achieve and create a vision that motivates them to achieve these goals.

Moreover, individuals possessing secure attachment styles benefit from caregivers' sensitivity and responsiveness to their needs, and tend to consider themselves as lovable, thus developing positive self-concept. This mechanism has also been suggested in sociometer theory of self-esteem (Leary, 1999) such that social acceptance and rejection is a determinant of one's self-esteem. More importantly, because when individuals realize that their actions can induce effective feedback from caregivers, they will also tend to develop a controllable view of the world with a higher sense of self-efficacy in mastering the environment. Individuals possessing secure attachment styles also tend to develop strong autonomous motivation in their interactions with caregivers because they are able to send their requests and receive appropriate responses from their caregivers in the knowledge that fulfilling their own needs is possible. Finally, positive interaction with caregivers reinforces positive emotion, fuelling such individuals with energy, not only because they feel satisfied with what they have received from their caregivers, but also because support from caregivers and the associated perceived self-competence help them overcome obstacles. A positive self-view, autonomous motivation and energy thus helps these individuals have higher expectations and be persistent in their pursuit of identified proactive goals.

Individuals with avoidant or ambivalent attachment styles are less likely to be proactive. Those with avoidant attachment styles are unable to obtain appropriate feedback from their caregivers, and may also be punished for expressing their needs. Consequently, they tend to protect themselves by keeping their distance from others, thus avoiding potential harm in social interactions (Cassidy and Kobak, 1988). Moreover, they have a greater desire to withdraw from exploration for fear of hurting others' feelings (Mikulincer, 1997). As such, they are not motivated to act on their curiosity and ultimately try to repress their unsatisfied curiosity (Mikulincer and Shaver, 2007a). Overall, they do not believe that they can use their actions to achieve what they want, and question the value of interacting with others and the external environment. Their withdrawal from interacting with others and the external environment in turn prevents them from identifying alternatives and opportunities to bring about change. As such, individuals with an avoidant attachment style are less likely to activate their proactive behavioural system.

The extent to which those with an ambivalent attachment style are proactive will depend on factors contingent on their ambivalence in social interactions. Those with ambivalent attachment styles tend to experience uncertain social environments, where caregivers do not always provide appropriate responses. Such individuals are still eager to pursue their goals as there is still hope that they will achieve them, but at the same time they question whether they will succeed in the end. Specifically, such individuals tend to develop a negative concept of the self as unlovable and incapable and intensify their distress experiences in order to increase attention and care from others (Wei et al, 2003). Their concept of self is more likely to be influenced by others' responses in social interactions, so their self-concept is less well defined (Wu, 2009) and their self-evaluation is vulnerable (Srivastava and Beer, 2005). Such individuals experience ambivalence in proactivity (Wu and Parker, 2012) as they experience feelings of mastery during exploration (Mikulincer, 1997) but do not perceive themselves as capable of sustaining such exploration or coping with potential distress (Wei et al, 2003). As such, the extent to which they engage in proactive behaviour will depend on the strength of their motivation for proactivity in a given situation and/or on the resources at hand to help them achieve it.

Based on above reasoning, I thus propose that individuals with a secure attachment style show the highest levels of proactivity, individuals with an avoidant attachment style show the lowest levels of proactivity, and those with an ambivalent attachment style are somewhere in the middle due to their ambivalence towards proactivity. Using a dimensional measure of attachment styles (attachment anxiety and attachment avoidance) (see Chapter Two for a discussion on the association between categorical and dimensional measures of attachment styles) and a measure of proactive personality to understand the association between attachment styles and individual differences in proactivity, one could therefore expect a stronger, negative association between attachment avoidance and proactivity personality (reflecting the differences in proactivity between those with secure versus avoidance attachment styles), and a negative but weaker association between attachment anxiety and proactivity personality (reflecting the differences in proactivity between those with secure versus ambivalent attachment styles). So far I have collected data from four samples from different backgrounds. To test this hypothesis, Table 5.1 presents results from the four samples. As the table shows, correlations vary across samples, and the hypothesis is supported in some samples but not all. As these samples are small, more studies would be needed to draw a firmer conclusion.

Table 5.1: Correlations between attachment styles and proactive personality

Sample	Characteristics of samples	Attachment anxiety	Attachment avoidance
Sample 1	90 employees from Taiwan	-.17	-.28**
Sample 2[a]	138 employees from the US	-.04	−.24**
Sample 3[a]	212 employees from China	.05	-.05
Sample 4[b]	179 employees from the Netherlands	.01	-.05

Notes:

a: Data for this sample has been published in Wu and Parker (2017).

b: Data for this sample has been published in Wu et al (2014).

** $p < .01$

Situational impact on proactivity

While attachment style – that is, a general sense of attachment security developed in early life – can determine an individual's general propensity towards proactivity, a sense of attachment security developed in relationships at work can be more proximal to influencing proactivity in the workplace. Although people may bring their original attachment prototype into a new relationship, they may revisit their perception of the relationship during subsequent interactions. As suggested in attachment theory, people can develop relationships with different targets, and it is possible to have a sense of attachment security in social relationships at work even if no such security exists in an individual's relationship with their caregiver. Such a possibility has been substantiated in attachment psychotherapy (Wallin, 2007). Moreover, empirical findings generally suggest that those with insecure attachment styles do not necessarily perceive deficiency in their relationships with their supervisors and others within the organization. For example, Schirmer and Lopez (2001) reported a null association between the two attachment dimensions (that is, attachment anxiety and attachment avoidance) and perceived supervisor support. Similarly, no association was found between attachment anxiety and perceived support from supervisors in two related studies by Wu and Parker (2017) or between attachment anxiety and perceived support from facilitators in a training context (Wang et al, 2018), although a weak negative association of attachment avoidance was obtained in Study 1 by Wu and Parker (2017) and by Wang and colleagues (2018). Accordingly, it is possible for managers or organizations to promote employee proactivity at work by enhancing employees' sense of attachment security at work.

The next section explores how supervisors, work groups and organizations – the three interaction targets at work from an employee's perspective – can promote employees' sense of attachment security and thus proactivity at work. The literature so far has indicated that supervisors (for example, Popper et al, 2000; Game, 2008; Wu and Parker, 2017), social groups (Smith et al, 1999) and organizations (Mayseless and Popper, 2007) can be viewed as attachment figures, and that employees can develop a sense of attachment security in their interactions with these different targets. As indicated by Bowlby (1997 [1969]), sensitivity and responsiveness to one's needs and readiness for social interaction are the main factors in establishing secure attachment, and supervisors, work groups and organizations that demonstrate these characteristics are likely to provide a secure base for employee exploration and proactivity. The next section elaborates how leadership, work team and organizational factors can contribute to building employees' sense of attachment security and thus promoting employee proactivity at work.

Leadership factors

As supervisors can directly influence employees' tasks, attitudes and behaviour at work, their ability to establish employees' sense of attachment security in their relationships will strongly affect employee proactivity at work. One direct leadership factor that helps establish employees' sense of attachment security with their supervisors is leader secure-base support (Wu and Parker, 2017). This concept is based on the Bowlby's (1988: 11) idea of secure base as 'one of being available, ready to respond when called upon to encourage and perhaps assist, but to intervene actively only when clearly necessary' and on Feeney and Thrush's (2010) elaboration of the three forms of support that jointly constitute secure-base support: availability, encouragement of growth and non-interference. Wu and Parker (2017: 1028–9, emphases in original) elaborate as follows:

> *Availability* refers to the extent to which the attachment figure is available when an individual is needed, such as to assist with removing obstacles. *Encouragement of growth* refers to the extent to which the attachment figure supports individual decisions and actions, and encourages an individual to achieve personal goals and to develop. *Noninterference* refers to the extent to which the attachment figure refrains from unnecessary interference with an individual's decisions and actions, such as by taking over an activity.

By offering all three forms of support, supervisors provide a secure base for employees to rely on to show their initiative and bring about changes at work.

Leader secure-base support can promote employee proactivity by facilitating employee goal envisioning and fuelling employees' self-regulation resources by enhancing positive self-concept, strengthening autonomous motivation and fuelling energy, which then contribute to goal regulation for achieving proactive goals. In brief, employees are more likely to think ahead and identify goals for improvement when they have encouragement from supervisors. Such encouragement without unnecessary interference persuades employees to believe that they have the competence to achieve their goals (Fisher et al, 1982; Bandura, 1999), cultivating a sense of self-efficacy. Secure-base support from supervisors also fosters employees' autonomous motivation, or a sense of volition in engaging in actions (Deci and Ryan, 1985), because it encourages employees to choose goals according to their interests (Sheldon and Elliot, 1999) without interference from supervisors and without the feeling that they are being externally controlled (Ryan and Deci, 2000). Finally, support from supervisors brings relational energy (that is, the psychological resources obtained from interactions with others) (Owens et al, 2016) as employees feel motivated and enthusiastic about tackling proactive goals when they have encouragement from supervisors and know they can approach them for help when facing obstacles or threats.

Empirical results from two studies by Wu and Parker (2017) show that leader secure-base support can strengthen one's self-efficacy (representing a 'can do' pathway) and autonomous motivation (representing a 'reason to' pathway), which in turn encourages employees to take initiatives, to bring about changes in the way they work. Across the two samples, Wu and Parker (2017) consistently found that leader secure-base support is more important for those with an insecure attachment style to engage in proactive behaviour at work. Specifically, leader secure-base support is more important for those high in attachment anxiety (or those with an ambivalent attachment style) to build a sense of self-efficacy, and is more important for those high in attachment avoidance (or those with an avoidant attachment style) to strengthen autonomous motivation, which in turn, contributes to a higher level of engagement in proactive work behaviour. This finding has two major implications. First, it suggests that employees with an insecure attachment style can actually enjoy secure-base support provided by their supervisors and be proactive in the workplace. Second, it indicates that employees with an insecure attachment style have different weaknesses (that is, lack of self-efficacy or lack of autonomous motivation) for not being proactive. Leader secure-base support helps different employees compensate for those weaknesses. Although Wu and Parker (2017) have reported finings to support the function of leader secure-base support on employee proactive behaviour via effects of self-efficacy and autonomous motivation, they did not examine whether leader secure-base support can facilitate employee goal envisioning, nor did they examine the role of energy, or an 'energized to' mechanism. As such, more studies are required to fully examine the proposed function and mechanisms of leader secure-base support in promoting employee proactivity at work.

In addition to the concept of leader secure-base support, there are leadership concepts from attachment theory that may have a role in establishing employees' sense of attachment security in leader–follower relationships. For example, transformational leadership has been suggested as a behavioural approach for establishing secure attachments between supervisors and their subordinates (Popper et al, 2000; Popper and Mayseless, 2003). Transformational leaders are those who aim to transform followers' attitudes, beliefs and values in order to achieve performance beyond expectations (Bass, 1985). To do so, such leaders create a vision that enables followers to conceive a different future, motivates followers using inspirational communication and challenges followers' work assumptions, while still treating each follower as an individual. Transformational leaders can promote followers' sense of attachment security for exploration in the workplace for two reasons. First, they explicitly encourage followers to think differently and try alternative ways to do their work. Second, they are able to establish a social and emotional bond with their followers by offering individualized support. As such, followers can approach their leader when needed. Empirically, transformational leadership has been consistently and positively associated with employee proactive behaviour (for example, Detert and Burris, 2007; Den Hartog and Belschak, 2012; Wu and Wang, 2015; Duan et al, 2017), but whether this association can be explained from an attachment theory perspective needs further examination.

Another relevant leadership concept is servant leadership (Greenleaf, 1977). In defining servant leadership, Greenleaf (1977: 13-14) makes the following argument:

> The servant leader is servant first.... It begins with the natural feeling that one wants to serve, to serve first. Then conscious choice brings one to aspire to lead.... The difference manifests itself in the care taken by the servant first to make sure that other people's highest priority needs are being served. The best test, and the most difficult to administer, is: Do those served grow as persons? Do they, while being served become healthier, wiser, freer, more autonomous, more likely themselves to become servants? And, what is the effect on the least privileged in society; will they benefit or, at least, not be further deprived?

In essence, the idea of servant leadership is very similar to the concept of secure base in terms of offering support for personal development when an individual is in need. It is thus very likely that servant leaders can establish securely attached relationships with their followers as they focus on satisfying the highest-priority needs of followers and offering resources and support to facilitate followers' personal and professional development. Similarly, servant leadership has been linked to employee proactive behaviour (for example, Panaccio et al, 2015), but whether such a link is established via employees' sense of attachment security in the leader–follower relationship needs further exploration.

Work team factors

Employees may attach to their work team, if the team is sensitive and responsive to their needs and offers support accordingly. To understand how team factors can play a role in building employees' sense of attachment security in teams, this section focuses on team climate – the shared perception of behaviours, practices and procedures within a team (West and Richter, 2011). A team climate that reflects positive social interactions within teams can help employees' develop a sense of attachment security.

Psychological safety, 'a shared belief that the team is safe for interpersonal risk taking' (Edmondson, 1999: 350), provides a social environment that allows employees to take the initiative and explore new ideas without worrying interpersonal risks such as being undermined or socially rejected. However, the concept of psychological safety only considers whether employees will be free from negative interpersonal consequences when taking the initiative, and not whether employees will have support and encouragement from their team to initiate change. As such, the concept of psychological safety is not comprehensive enough to fully capture the idea of secure base and thus is not strong enough to establish employees' sense of attachment security in teams. In this regard, a 'high care' team atmosphere (Von Krogh, 1998; Zárraga and Bonache, 2005) characterized by mutual trust, active empathy, lenience in judgment, courage and access to help should serve a more active role in developing employees' sense of attachment security in teams, as in these circumstances employees enjoy encouragement and support from the team to explore new ideas and try alternative approaches to their work.

So far psychological safety at the team level has been found to positively associate with employees' voice behaviour at the individual level (Walumbwa and Schaubroeck, 2009), but the effect of high care team atmosphere has not been studied. Empirical studies are also needed to directly examine the mechanism of attachment security in work teams when investigating the effect of team psychological safety and high care team atmosphere on employee proactive behaviour.

Organizational factors

Employees may attach to their organization by viewing the organization as an interaction partner that possesses human characteristics. For example, in a review of studies on employees' perception of organizational support, Rhoades and Eisenberger (2002: 711) indicated that 'employees personify the organization, infer the extent to which the organization values their contributions and cares about their well-being, and reciprocate such perceived support with increased commitment, loyalty, and performance'. Ashforth and Rogers (2012: 31) also suggest that 'Organizations are not people, yet they are routinely endowed with human-like characteristics to make them more comprehensible to insiders and outsiders alike.... This process is called anthropomorphization'. Following this, employees can view their organizations as human-like and as having a choice in how they treat employees, providing a basis for employees to develop a sense of attachment security in their relationships with the organization.

To understand how organizations can build up employees' sense of attachment security, I focus on two concepts – perceived organizational support and psychological contracts – that have been used to understand the employee–organization relationship. Although these two concepts are usually understood from a social exchange perspective, whereby employees will exchange their effort, performance and proactivity for support or promises from their organization (Coyle-Shapiro and Conway, 2005; Coyle-Shapiro and Shore, 2007), I argue that these two concepts can be viewed from an attachment theory perspective. In brief, I suggest that by offering perceived organizational support and supportive psychological contract, organizations can serve as a secure base for employee exploration and proactivity, which represents an enabling mechanism. This is different from the social exchange perspective that emphasizes the role of felt obligation in exchange in explaining why perceived organizational support and supportive psychological contract can promote employee proactivity.

Perceived organizational support can be defined as 'employees' general belief that their work organization values their contribution and cares about their well-being' (Rhoades and Eisenberger, 2002: 698). This concept can be used to gauge whether employees view their organization as an attachment figure for exploration as it directly captures employee perception of the support they need from their organization. However, perceived organizational support is a very broad concept that includes support in many dimensions. For example, Eisenberger and colleagues (1986) developed a scale to assess employees' perceived organizational support by including items concerning performance recognition (that is, 'the organization takes pride in my accomplishments at work') and items reflecting secure-base support ('the organization strongly considers my goals and values; help is available from the organization when I have a problem; the organization is willing to extend itself in order to help me perform my job to the best of my ability'). Although employees will have an overall perception of organizational support, it would be more effective to establish employees' sense of attachment security in the employee–organization relationship by offering secure-base support instead of other types of support.

While the concept of perceived organizational support captures employees' perception, the psychological contract is the concept that helps capture the relationship between employees and their organization. Psychological contracts refer to 'an individual's beliefs regarding the terms and conditions of a reciprocal exchange agreement between the focal person and another party' (Rousseau, 1989: 123) that 'serve to bind together individuals and organisations and regulate their behaviour, making possible the achievement of organizational goals' (Robinson et al, 1994: 137). Organizations can develop different psychological contracts with their employees. Rousseau (1995) and Rousseau and Wade-Benzoni (1994) have differentiated between three types of psychological contract: transactional, relational and balanced psychological contracts. Transactional psychological contract is characterized by a short-term employment relationship in which performance requirements or mutual obligations are clearly specified. Relational psychological contract is characterized by long-term employment relationships in which mutual obligations are less specified. Balanced psychological contract is characterized by long-term employment relationships in which the performance requirements or mutual obligations are clearly specified; it can be regarded as a combination of the relational and transactional contracts – 'an open-ended relational emphasis with the transactional feature of well specified performance-reward contingencies' (Hui et al 2004: 312).

From an attachment perspective, relational psychological contract is seemingly the best one to help employees develop a sense of attachment security as it supports a long-term relationship between employee and the organization without performance-related, conditional requirements. However, having relational psychological contracts between employees and the organizations does not necessarily mean that organizations will actively encourage and support employees to explore and be proactive. In other words, having relational psychological contracts would not be strong enough for employees to view their organization as a secure base for being proactive. In this regard, adding components regarding learning and development to the relational psychological contracts would be more effective in encouraging a sense of attachment security and enabling employees to try different things at work. Establishing a balanced psychological contract could thus be helpful in this regard if the specified performance-reward contingencies can serve a function to encourage employees to achieve goals and facilitate personal development.

Although it is possible for organizations to promote employees' sense of attachment security by offering organizational support and building relational or balanced psychological contract, there is a challenge for organizations to manage and shape employees' perception of organizational support and their understanding of psychological contract (Coyle-Shapiro and Parzefall, 2008). Organizations are not real persons and employees actually build their relationships with the organizations via interactions with those who represent the organizations, which could be immediate and senior managers. Moreover, employees can develop different psychological contracts with different interaction targets (that is, supervisors, colleagues, and so on) in the organization (Alcover et al, 2017). As such, whether employees would have a sense of attachment security in their relationships with their organization via the function of perceived organizational support and psychological contracts specifically can be determined by multiple players in the organization at the interpersonal level. As such, building employees' sense of attachment security in employee–organization relationships will rely on collective effort from multiple interaction targets.

Summary

This chapter has explored why there are individual differences in proactivity and how different sectors (that is, leaders, work teams and organizations) can promote employee proactivity at work based on the function of attachment security in facilitating the operation of behavioural system of proactivity as proposed in Chapter Four. This chapter demonstrates how we can use the proposed model in Chapter Four to understand dispositional and situational forces in shaping proactivity from a different angle. Chapter Six examines broader implications of applying attachment theory to understand proactivity and indicates directions for future research.

SIX

Implications for Employee Proactivity Research

Research on proactivity has so far mainly considered proactivity as an individual's action and used a sell-regulation perspective to understand employee proactive behaviour at work. Nevertheless, proactivity is very often relational, in part because it is often necessary to manage disapproval and resistance from other stakeholders in the work context (Morrison and Bies, 1991; Frese and Fay, 2001; Ashford et al, 2003; Parker et al, 2010). Similarly, when behaving proactively, an individual often needs to interact closely with and influence peers and supervisors in order to obtain the information and resources needed to bring about change (Thompson, 2005). As such, the extent to which employees are proactive is determined by how they interact with other stakeholders in the work context. Building on attachment theory, this book has proposed that attachment security is the key that activates and facilitates operation of the behavioural system of proactivity (Chapter Four) and suggested that attachment styles and different stakeholders in the work context (that is, leaders, work teams and the organization) can be sources of attachment security in shaping employee proactivity at work (Chapter Five).

The aim of this chapter is to highlight the implications for employee proactivity research of the model proposed in Chapters Four and Five. First, the chapter discusses how attachment theory provides a different angle from alternative approaches for understanding the relational basis of employee proactivity. Next, it elaborates how the attachment theory strengthens a dispositional approach to understanding employee proactivity, and then highlights the value of the proposed model in integrating the different conceptualizations and motivational mechanisms in proactivity research. Finally, it indicates avenues for future research on employee proactivity specifically and extends the discussion to elaborate how attachment theory can help understand work behaviour broadly.

Relational basis of employee proactivity

Although different approaches can be adopted capture the relational basis of proactivity, the approach in this book, of building on attachment theory, provides a stronger theoretical foundation for unpacking the relational basis of proactivity. For example, in order to examine whether those who tend to build positive relationships with others will be more proactive at work, previous studies have examined the association between trait agreeableness from the 'big-five' personality framework (i.e., a trait theory of personality focusing on the five broad traits – conscientiousness, agreeableness, neuroticism, openness, and extraversion) and employee proactive behaviour (for example, LePine and Van Dyne, 2001; Major et al, 2006; Crant et al, 2011). Those high in trait agreeableness are sympathetic, cooperative and warm and are more likely to build positive relationships and accumulate social capital at work for initiating change. The association between trait agreeableness employee proactive behaviour is weak, which could be due to the fact that agreeableness is a broad or superordinate trait that includes specific traits such as altruism, compliance and trust that are not specific to how an individual perceives or feels in social relationships. Moreover, the big-five personality framework does not provide an answer for why people with certain traits are more likely to engage in proactive behaviour. Clustering traits into a broader personality construct and imposing a name on it does not provide a rigorous theoretical explanation for why certain personality constructs link to certain types of behaviour, such as proactive behaviour. By contrast, attachment theory provides a concept of attachment style that directly captures an individual's perception and feelings in a specific relationship and offers a theoretical account for why individuals with different attachment styles tend to be more or less proactive.

Previous studies have also adopted a social exchange perspective to capture the relational component of proactivity (for example, Fuller et al, 2006; Lam et al, 2007; Bal et al, 2011; Yusuf, 2017). The main idea is that employees engage in proactive behaviour and take initiative as a means to exchange benefits or support with supervisors or organizations. As a way of understanding the relational basis of proactivity, the social exchange approach is different from the attachment approach in several ways. First, the basic assumption relating to the relationship between employees and supervisors or organizations is different. While the social exchange approach assumes a conditional relationship between employees and supervisors or organizations in which employees exchange their initiatives for support and benefits from supervisors or organizations, the attachment approach emphasizes unconditional support from supervisors or organizations for employees to explore and take the initiative.

Second, the two approaches differ in the underlying mechanisms explaining why employees engage in proactive behaviour. A social exchange approach concerns exchange between two parties, suggesting that individuals engage in proactive behaviour for a reason, in brief, to gain something from the other party. In contrast, the attachment approach emphasizes the function of attachment security in cultivating an individual's exploration desire and behavior, and thus suggests that individuals engage in proactive behaviour because they are enabled to do so. As such, I would argue that the social exchange approach will only help develop a temporary relational basis for fostering employee proactivity as employees may not engage in proactive behaviour when they cannot obtain benefits or what they value from the other party. The attachment approach will help develop a permanent relational basis for fostering employee proactivity as employees will be motivated to explore as long as they feel a sense of attachment security.

Finally, the two approaches also differ in terms of proactivity target. The social exchange approach, based on the idea of reciprocity, argues that employees will engage in proactive behaviour to bring benefits only to those who have given them support. In other words, the social exchange approach suggests target-specific proactivity, such that employees will engage in proactive behaviour towards their supervisor, work team or organization depending on who specifically gives them resources, benefits or recognition in the exchange relationship. The attachment approach does not suggest target-specific proactivity. Although an individual can develop a sense of attachment security in different relationship contexts, the function of attachment security in facilitating proactivity is not target-specific. Under the attachment approach, it is possible to see a spillover effect such that employees can develop a sense of attachment security in their relationship with the supervisors and thus engage in proactive behaviour for improving their own work (in other words, proactive work behaviour), career (proactive career behaviour) or the organization directly (proactive strategic behaviour) (Parker and Collins, 2010). In sum, attachment theory offers a different lens from the social exchange perspective to unpack the relational basis of employee proactivity.

Dispositional foundation of proactivity

While offering a theoretical account to underpin the relational basis of proactivity, attachment theory also offers a developmental account to explain individual differences in proactivity. Although the concept of proactive personality has been proposed to recognize individual differences in proactivity, there is no explanation for why people differ in their proactive personalities. Attachment theory fills this gap and suggests that people can develop different levels of proactivity based on their interaction experiences with primary caregivers in early life.

Not only does attachment theory offer a theoretical foundation to underpin individual differences in proactivity, but it also provides a different approach to understanding the association between personality and proactivity, an even boarder theoretical contribution to proactivity research.

Perspectives of personality can in general be divided into two types: the structure view and the process view (Fleeson, 2001). The structure view of personality aims to find elements that can describe an individual's stable characteristics. Trait theory is an example of this view. The process view treats personality as a dynamic system and aims to understand the characterized operation of the system of an individual. The psycho–analysis paradigm and its associated theories, such as attachment theory, are examples of this view. Although these two views are not exclusive and have been integrated with Fleeson's two-level model approach (Fleeson, 2001; Fleeson and Gallagher, 2009; Minbashian et al, 2010), the structure view of personality focusing on traits is dominant in work behaviour literature and, of course, in the literature on proactive behaviour. So far many dispositional antecedents of proactive behaviour, such as proactive personality, the dimensions of big-five personality and other specific traits (see Wu et al, 2013), have been identified under the structure view.

An apparent challenge to the structure view of personality is how to find a framework to organize different traits and depict their underlying mechanisms in shaping proactive behaviour. The big-five personality framework is an obvious choice, and it has been applied to understand proactive behaviour in several studies (for example, LePine and Van Dyne, 2001; Major et al, 2006; Crant et al, 2011). Despite the fact that the big-five personality framework is well-established and incorporates a lot of personality traits, it does not cover other dispositional constructs such as proactive personality or need for cognition, which are distinct, have unique effects, and require a different theoretical path for predicting and shaping proactive behaviour. Also, the big-five personality framework does not provide theoretical explanations for why people with certain traits are more likely to engage in proactive behaviour, as mentioned earlier. To address the limitation of the big-five personality framework, Wu and colleagues (2013) seek to use a 'functional classification of personality' (Buss and Finn, 1987) to summarize dispositional traits that can predict proactive behaviour.

The functional classification conceives of personality traits as cognitive, affective and instrumental, according to their unique functions of, respectively, reflecting beliefs and understanding, expressing emotional response to and governing behaviours to interact with the environment. Corresponding to these aspects, Buss and Finn (1987) discovered that cognitive traits involve behaviours that have a strong component of thoughts, imagination and information processing (for example, openness to experience is a cognitive trait because it is associated with an increased tendency to consider unconventional or unfamiliar ideas); affective traits involve behaviours that have a strong emotional component (for example, neuroticism is an affective trait due to its association with increased experience and expression of negative, distressing emotions); and instrumental traits involve behaviours that have an impact on the environment (for example, assertiveness is an instrumental trait because it is associated with an increased tendency to speak up, lead others and force others to accept one's opinions). As such, in contrast to the big-five personality framework, which classifies personality traits according to their content (John et al, 2008), functional classification classifies personality traits according to how they influence behaviour. Based on this functional classification of personality, Wu and colleagues (2013) suggest that cognitive traits (such as openness to experience, curiosity, future orientation and need for cognition) contribute to proactivity in the workplace because they enhance the likelihood that an individual will recognize opportunities and generate ideas for the future; affective traits (such as positive affectivity and negative affectivity) contribute to proactivity because these traits increase the experience of energy to purse more challenging goals; and finally, instrumental traits (such as proactive personality and generalized self-efficacy) likely contribute to proactivity in the workplace because these traits imply a strong tendency toward mastering the environment. In this way, Wu and colleagues (2013) suggest an alternative framework of personality traits to explicitly show the functions of traits that shape proactive behaviour.

Although functional classification of personality compensates for the weakness of the structural view of personality, especially the trait paradigm, by considering underlying mechanisms of personality traits, how personality is developed and interacts with environment, which reflects the process view of personality, has not been theorized or considered. In fact, the way in which the process view of personality can help understand motivational mechanisms in shaping proactive behaviour is demonstrated in Chapters Four and Five, where attachment theory is used to understand proactive behaviour. As elaborated in Chapter One, attachment theory is developed from psychoanalysis paradigms and suggests that within an individual, there are several goal-corrected behavioural systems that operate together to shape an individual's behaviour and that, among these behavioural systems, the attachment behavioural system is the central system that plays a dominant role in influencing the operation of other behavioural systems. Thus, attachment theory is in line with a process of personality theory because it treats personality as a dynamic system and aims to understand the operational process in the whole system. In this way, personality is the individualized characteristics in operating the system (Mischel and Shoda,

1995). For example, in attachment theory, an attachment style is the stable individual characteristic involved in operating the attachment behavioural system and thus results in a specific pattern in governing other behavioural systems (for example, the exploration/proactive behavioural system) and behaviours (for example, proactive behaviour). As such, attachment theory draws on a process view of personality to understand the dispositional foundation of proactivity and underlying motivational mechanisms.

Integration of different conceptualizations and motivational mechanisms of proactivity

In addition to the contributions outlined in the previous section, attachment theory provides a theoretical framework to integrate different conceptualizations and motivational mechanisms of proactivity reviewed in Chapter One. These different conceptualizations and motivational mechanisms of proactivity have been proposed independently in proactivity literature, adding different elements to understanding proactivity as a whole. Although that knowledge has deepened our overall understanding of proactivity, a lack of an integrative framework has left a patchwork of proactivity research. Attachment theory helps fill the gaps, as these different conceptualizations and motivational mechanisms of proactivity can be incorporated through the lens of attachment theory.

As reviewed in Chapter One, proactivity has been understood from dispositional, behavioural and process perspectives. These three perspectives can be fully integrated through a lens of attachment theory, which provides the concept of attachment styles to explain individual differences in proactivity and offers the concept of behavioural system to delineate the goal-regulatory process (that is, envisioning, planning, performance and reflection) in governing different types of proactive behaviour under the same system. In addition, attachment theory provides a theoretical basis for suggesting how attachment security can facilitate goal envisioning and bring self-regulation resources to facilitate the operation of the behavioural system of proactivity via the function of goal expectancy, goal importance and regulatory energy, which reflects 'can do', 'reason to' and 'energized to' motivational mechanism respectively (Parker et al, 2010). As such, attachment theory helps integrate knowledge we have so far to understand proactivity.

The integration of knowledge in proactivity research is important because it enables us to see how different conceptualizations and motivational mechanisms of proactivity can be tied together, which helps not only summarize what we already know but also indicate research avenues that can be further explored, as elaborated in the next section.

Future research on employee proactivity

This section suggests several research avenues for future studies on employee proactivity. As empirical evidence is needed to support the validity of the proposed model to explain employee proactive behaviour, the first and most direct area of future research is to test the model and propositions elucidated in Chapters Four and Five.

To properly examine the operation of the behavioural system of proactivity – a behavioural system that can operate differently depending on individuals' attachment styles – future research should adopt a two-level approach to personality to delineate how employees with different attachment styles (that is, variation at the between-individual level) operate their behavioural system of proactivity differently (that is, variation at the within-individual level). Fleeson (2001) and Fleeson and Gallagher (2009) proposed a two-level model – 'between-individual' and 'within-individual' levels – to achieve this purpose. Fleeson suggests theorizing personality as a two-level system, in which we can identify dispositions at the between-individual level to acknowledge differences across individuals in terms of their personality structure, and specify associations between stimuli, psychological states, experiences or behaviour at the within-individual level to describe the operational function and process in each individual's personality system. In this way, researchers can identify which dispositions are important for shaping certain behaviours via which internal mechanisms in the personality system. This is also a way of integrating the structure view and the process view of personality as discussed earlier.

So far Wu and Parker (2012) have conducted a study using the two-level approach. In a monthly survey study, the authors found that state core self-evaluations, state curiosity and state future orientation in a given month positively predicted proactive behaviour in that month at the within-individual level. They also reported that people high in attachment anxiety at the between-individual level tend not to rely on their state self-evaluations to pursue a proactive action at a given time, but that they tend to engage in such behaviour when they have a stronger future goal at a given time. These findings in general reflect the ambivalent attitude of anxiously attached individuals toward external worlds such that they acknowledge feelings of mastery during exploration (Mikulincer, 1997), but do not perceive themselves as being capable of sustaining this exploration or coping with potential difficulty or subsequent distress (Wei et al, 2003). As the findings show, although such individuals would like to achieve future goals via proactive behaviour, at the same time, the fragility of their self-concept does not help them sustain proactive actions. The study also found that attachment avoidance and proactive personality at the between-individual level had no cross-level interaction effect to moderate the relationships among variables at the within-individual level. Although the study did not directly test the model proposed here, it demonstrates how we can adopt a two-level model approach to examine the individual differences in the operation of the behavioural system of proactivity at within-individual level.

In addition to a direct examination of the proposed model, future research could elaborate on issues raised in this book relating to the characteristics of leaders, work teams and organizations that provide employees with attachment security. Although this book has discussed the role of leaders, work teams and organizations, and indicated several characteristics of each that may promote employee attachment security, there are more questions to tackle. The remainder of this section elaborates on this, first with regard to leadership, and then work teams and organizations.

In terms of leadership, this book has not spent much time addressing which leaders are more likely to provide secure-base support and which combination of leaders and followers best establishes a leader–follower secure attachment relationship. These two issues are addressed here from the perspective of attachment theory. First, one interesting avenue for future research would be to explore which types of supervisor are most likely to provide secure-base support. Identifying the attributes of supervisors who are more likely to provide secure-base support, such as motivational, contextual or dispositional factors, would have implications for determining ways to use the leadership system to enhance employee proactive behaviour at work. Attachment theory provides a potentially useful lens through which to examine this issue because attachment style has been shown to be associated with caregiving behaviour, such that people with higher attachment security are more sensitive and responsive to others' needs (Mikulincer and Shaver, 2005; Collins and Ford, 2010). Accordingly, supervisors with attachment styles reflecting higher attachment security might be more likely to provide secure-base support to their subordinates, and thus enhance employee proactive behaviour at work.

Several empirical findings in close relationships studies or leadership studies have provided preliminary support for such speculation. For example, in a close relationships context, Collins and Feeney (2000) found that attachment anxiety was associated with less instrumental support, less responsiveness and more negative caregiving behaviour. In another study, Feeney and Collins (2001) reported that attachment anxiety was positively associated with compulsive caregiving (as identified by the statement 'creating problems by taking on my partner's troubles as if they were my own') and controlling caregiving ('being too domineering when trying to help my partner'), while attachment avoidance was negatively associated with responsive caregiving (for example, 'when my partner is having a problem, I try to provide reassurance that everything will be okay'). The authors further identified that having social support knowledge, higher interdependence and trust in relationships, as well as being pro-socially oriented and not egoistic-oriented, are factors contributing to why people with higher attachment security provide more responsive caregiving and less compulsive and controlling caregiving. Similarly, Feeney and Thrush (2010) reported that attachment avoidance is negatively associated with support for availability and attachment anxiety is negatively associated with non-interference and encouragement – the other two components in secure-base support. These findings may suggest that supervisors with higher attachment security (that is, lower attachment anxiety and lower attachment avoidance) can provide appropriate support for employees to be proactive. This speculation also correlates with findings in leadership studies, where individuals with high attachment security are more likely to be nominated for leadership positions in a military context (Popper et al, 2004), whereas leaders with insecure attachment tend to adopt a leadership style that focuses on their own personal needs and is less pro-social (Popper, 2002; Davidovitz et al, 2007). Thus, in future studies, we can use the theoretical attachment–caregiving association to understand which leaders are more likely to encourage employee proactive behaviour by providing secure-base support.

Taking supervisors' attachment styles into account also helps us explore how the dyadic dynamics in leader–follower relationships shape employee proactive behaviour from a leader–follower relationship perspective of leadership, a second potential area for future research. Keller (2003) touched on this issue in a conceptual paper, in which she drew on implicit leadership theory and proposed that congruence between leaders and followers' attachment styles (a securely attached employee with a securely attached supervisor or an avoidantly attached employee with an avoidantly attached supervisor) will result in better leader–follower relationships. In contrast to Keller's approach, which fully relies on implicit leadership theory with an emphasis on the consistency of mutual expectation, the following paragraphs review empirical findings in adult attachment literature and use these findings to propose a different set of ideas about how different combinations of leader and follower attachment styles can shape the quality of leader–follower relationships. As presented and elaborated shortly, existing findings do not fully support Keller's congruence hypothesis.

The studies reviewed here are those conducted by Collins and Feeney (2000), Feeney and Thrush (2010) and Richards and Hackett (2012). Although the first two studies focus on interaction within romantic couples, their paradigms and findings can help us examine the dyadic dynamics in leader–follower relationships.

Collins and Feeney (2000) examined the dynamic of the support-seeking process and caregiving process in 93 dating couples and found that both partners' attachment styles jointly shaped the relationship quality through their support-seeking and caregiving behaviour. Using a laboratory paradigm, Collins and Feeney (2000) videotaped romantic couples while one member of the couple disclosed a stressful problem to the other, so that one partner played the role of support seeker and the other of caregiver. Using independent observers to rate support-seeking behaviour and caregiving behaviour, in general they found that 'individuals who rated their problem as more stressful engaged in more direct support-seeking behaviour, which in turn was associated with more effective caregiving responses from their partner. These caregiving responses were then linked to the support seeker's subjective experience of support, which predicted improvements in the support seeker's mood' (Collins and Feeney, 2000: 1067). The authors also found that caregivers who had higher satisfaction with their relationships were more responsive and provided more emotional support and less negative support, and support seekers who had higher satisfaction with their relationships had partners who were better caregivers overall, indicating that 'caregivers and support seekers who were involved in better-functioning relationships had interactions in which the caregiver was rated as being more caring and supportive' (Collins and Feeney: 1065). Bringing the attachment styles of both members of the couple into account, they further indicated that support seekers with higher attachment avoidance tended to have ineffective supporting-seeking behaviour and caregivers with higher attachment anxiety tended to have ineffective caregiving behaviour. Their findings thus imply that a combination of avoidantly attached support seekers and anxiously attached caregivers would lead to an ineffective relationship exchange.

Feeney and Thrush (2010) recruited 167 married couples and randomly assigned each member of the couple to the role of either 'explorer' or 'spouse' in a puzzle-solving task that was novel and challenging to the participants. They videotaped the explorer and spouse interaction and focused on the explorer's exploration behaviour in terms of performance, expressed confidence in self, persistence and enthusiasm in doing the task, and the spouse's secure-base behaviour in terms of availability, non-interference and encouragement. In general, they found that the spouse's secure-base behaviour positively contributed to the explorer's exploration behaviour, enjoyment in doing the task, and positive view toward the spouse, including less negativity/

hostility, more positive affect toward the spouse, and willingness to seek encouragement/emotional support from the spouse. This finding suggests that secure-base support can help couples form effective relationships in facing novel and challenging tasks. More importantly, Feeney and Thrush (2010) further indicated that spouses who were high in attachment avoidance were less likely to be available to support and respond to explorers' requests, and spouses high in attachment anxiety tended to interfere with explorers' actions and give less encouragement. Explorers high in attachment avoidance or attachment anxiety tended not to perceive their spouses as being available, and explorers high in attachment avoidance tended not to think of their spouses as being encouraging. Because spouse's secure-base support (that is, availability, non-interference and encouragement) played an important role in promoting explorers' exploration behaviour and, potentially, their relationship quality, findings related to attachment styles therefore suggest that the combination of insecurely attached spouses and insecurely attached explorers leads to an ineffective relationship, especially in the face of novel and challenging tasks.

In brief, Collins and Feeney (2000) and Feeney and Thrush (2010) demonstrated that considering the attachment styles of both members of a couple can help understand the conditions under which an effective relationship is more likely to be established in the face of pressure or challenging tasks. However, their findings do not provide solid evidence as they did not directly test the interaction effect between the attachment styles of the two members in the couple. Moreover, although attachment styles will influence individuals' social relationships in general, the findings obtained regarding close relationships may not be directly applicable to leader–follower relationships, as these two types of relationships are different in many ways, for example, in that there is a clear hierarchy and unequal power resources in leader–follower relationships, and leader–follower relationships are based more for instrumental reasons, such as achieving a specific goal in an organization by playing specific roles. Hence, a direct study focusing on how leaders' and followers' attachment styles shape the leader–follower relationships is required.

Recently, Richards and Hackett (2012) conducted research directly examining the interaction effect between leaders' and followers' attachment styles in predicating leader–member exchange (LMX). They found that an individual's attachment anxiety (either a leader's or a follower's) was negatively associated with LMX reported by the individual, but this negative association was mitigated when the partner (either a follower or a leader) had higher attachment anxiety. Specific findings are that LMX is highest when both members in the leader–follower dyad have low attachment anxiety and that LMX is lowest when only one of the members in the leader–follower dyad has high attachment anxiety. There was no significant interaction effect when attachment avoidance was analyzed. Based on this report, therefore, Keller's congruence hypothesis is not fully supported. However, Richards and Hackett (2012) did not further examine which types of behaviour exhibited leaders or followers led to a good LMX and whether the LMX would mediate the association between attachment styles and proactive behaviour at a dyadic level. Further studies are therefore required to extend research on attachment styles and proactive behaviour into a dyadic context by taking both leaders' and followers' attachment styles, behaviour and relationship experiences into account.

The same sets of question for leadership can be applied to research on work teams and organizations: which teams or organizations are more likely to provide support to promote employee attachment security, and what combination of employees and their work teams or organizations best establishes a secure attachment relationship with the teams or the organizations? To my knowledge, there is no relevant study so far that addresses these two questions, as attachment-related studies mainly focus on interpersonal interactions. Accordingly, they are totally new areas for exploration. Addressing these questions will need input from studies on team research and organization studies in addition to those on attachment theory, denoting the needs and the opportunities of integrating different disciplines to generate new understandings of employee proactivity. Understanding how teams and organizations shape employee proactive behaviour at the individual level will also help unpack a multi-level understanding of employee proactivity *beyond* the individual level.

Application of attachment theory to work behaviour

The previous sections have discussed how attachment theory can help us understand employee proactivity, and have proposed potential areas for more research. This section discusses how attachment theory can help us understand work behaviour more broadly. It focuses specifically on the concept of the 'goal-corrected behavioural system' proposed in attachment theory because the operation principle of a behavioural system and the behavioural systems reviewed in Chapter Two can help describe the motivational systems behind different types of work behaviour (such as helping, mentoring or innovation) that have been widely discussed in organizational behaviour literature.

In organizational behaviour literature, work behaviour has been classified according to its purpose and function at work. In general, work behaviour can be classified into three board categories as suggested by Rotundo and Sackett (2002), which include task performance; behaviour aimed at accomplishing the requirements of a job; citizenship performance or organizational citizenship behaviour (OCB); behaviour that is discretionary and not directly related to job requirement but that promotes the effective functioning of the organization; and counterproductive performance or counterproductive work behaviour (CWB), which is voluntary behaviour that goes against the effective functioning of an organization. Although this classification summarizes various forms of behaviour at work, it is limited in its ability to provide a specific understanding of each behaviour. For example, in their review on the concept of OCB, Podsakoff and colleagues (2000: 516) indicate that 'almost 30 potentially different forms of citizenship behaviour have been identified', and summarize them into seven broad concepts, including helping behaviour, sportsmanship, organizational loyalty, organizational compliance, individual initiative, civic virtue, and self-development. The same issue and approach has been applied to the concept of CWB (Robinson and Bennett, 1995; Sackett et al, 2006). Therefore, a challenge of this framework is to understand the antecedents and motivational mechanisms of each specific behaviour within this classification. For example, helping behaviour and voice behaviour have both been regarded as forms of OCB, but they have contrasting meanings in terms of affiliative or promotive motivation and differential relationships with the big-five personality traits (Van Dyne and LePine, 1998; LePine and Van Dyne, 2001). This example shows that the three-classification framework cannot specify behaviours homogeneously. On the other hand, like the big-five personality framework in classifying traits into broad constructs, the classification of work behaviours based on their broader functions or valence (positive or negative) does not help link motivations or the underlying mechanisms behind those behaviours. This is the reason why research must find another theoretical framework in motives to depict individuals' motivations in engaging in certain work behaviour (for example, Rioux and Penner, 2001).

In order to understand more of the mechanisms of work behaviour, I propose using Bowlby's (1997 [1969]) concept of a 'goal-corrected behavioural system' to provide a different approach to classifying work behaviour (see Chapter Two for more details). Focusing on attachment, caregiving, affiliation, and power behavioural systems (see Table 2.1 for their inherent features), here I provide the preliminary classification of different work behaviours based on these behavioural systems. For example, work behaviour that aims to obtain care and helps from others, such as support or help seeking at work, is governed by the attachment behavioural system. This classification is reasonable as many previous studies in adult attachment literature have theorized that support or help seeking in adulthood is governed by the attachment behavioural system (for example, Florian et al, 1995; Collins and Feeney, 2000; Collins and Ford, 2010). Supporting this view, Richards and Schat (2011) reported that attachment anxiety is positively related to support seeking at work, whereas attachment avoidance is negatively related to support seeking at work, revealing that hyperactivating the attachment behavioural system (for those high in attachment anxiety) will increase support-seeking behaviour at work whereas deactivating the attachment behavioural system (for those high in attachment avoidance) will decrease support-seeking behaviour at work.

Work behaviour aimed at helping others confront danger or stress or pursue challenging goals is governed by the caregiving behavioural system. This classification is also reasonable since studies in adult attachment literature have theorized that providing help and support is governed by this type of behavioural system (for example, Collins and Feeney, 2000; Feeney and Collins, 2001; Mikulincer et al, 2005; Collins and Ford, 2010). Popper and Mayseless (2003) also touch on this issue by applying a parenting perspective in caregiving to understand transformational leadership. Together these ideas suggest that the caregiving behavioural system governs various behaviours such as the helping behaviour towards peers described in OCB literature or the support behaviour described in leadership and mentorship literature. Geller and Bamberger (2009) have used attachment theory to understand helping behaviour at work. They found that people high in attachment avoidance have lower 'helping depth', as their peers reported receiving less support from them, and people high in attachment anxiety have lower 'helping breadth', as only a small proportion of their peers reported having been helped by them. This finding is consistent with the notion that a deficiency in operating the attachment behavioural system (for those high in attachment anxiety or attachment avoidance) will lead to the dysfunction of the caregiving behavioural system as theorized in attachment theory.

I further propose that behaviour aimed at jointly facing challenges or averting threats, such as cooperating with others or showing organizational loyalty, is governed by the affiliation behavioural system. However, to date, the affiliation behavioural system has not yet been widely examined in attachment literature. There are no related empirical findings in a work context that can support this speculation.

I further contend that behaviour aimed at protecting resources and exhibiting ability for the sake of gaining influence at work, such as sabotage behaviour, a form of counterproductive work behaviour, is governed by the power behavioural system. Shaver and colleagues (2011) recently proposed that the power behavioural system can be used to explain how individuals behave in situations that influence their sense of power, and thus their behavioural and emotional responses (such as hostility and aggression). Without linking the power behavioural system to the attachment behavioural system, Shaver and colleagues developed a measure for assessing a dispositional characteristic in operating the power behavioural system (for example, hyperactivate or deactivate) and used this measure to predict aggressive behaviour.

Based on the discussion here and on very preliminary classification, one suggestion for future study would be to use Bowlby's (1997 [1969]) concept of a 'goal-corrected behavioural system' to provide a different approach to classifying work behaviour. This approach would have three important contributions. First, it directly theorizes the mechanisms of certain work behaviours by describing when a behavioural system will be activated and by identifying the end goal the system aims to achieve. It helps understand the antecedents and functions of a certain work behaviour. Second, these identified behavioural systems serve different biological functions from an ecological perspective, which suggests that these systems are fundamental to human beings in guiding individual behaviour and maximizing the likelihood of survival. As such, relying on these identified behavioural systems to classify and investigate different types of work behaviour can strengthen the theoretical understanding of the basic human motivations that shape work behaviour. Finally, as discussed previously, a goal-corrected behavioural system can be treated as a personality system, its operational characteristics reflecting an individual characteristic that differentiates one individual from another. Therefore, the goal-corrected behavioural system approach links personality, mechanisms and behaviour together, providing a more comprehensive and integrative approach to explaining work behaviour.

Coda

People who are proactive envision a better future and take action to achieve it. They should be confident, motivated and energetic, as it is not always easy to bring about change. Being supported in relationships with surrounding others is the greatest aid to such courage. This book has adopted an attachment theory perspective to understand the relational basis of employee proactivity, and has elaborated how such theoretical perspective can advance our understanding of employee' proactive behaviour or work behaviour more broadly.

References

Ainsworth, M. D. S. (1990) 'Epilogue: Some considerations of attachment theory and assessment relevant to the years beyond infancy', in Greenberg, M. T., Cicchetti, D. and Cummings, E. M., eds., *Attachment in the pre-school years: Theory, research, and intervention*, Chicago, IL: University of Chicago Press, 463-488.

Ainsworth, M. D. S., Blehar, M. C., Waters, E. and Wall, S. (1978) *Patterns of attachment: A psychological study of the strange situation*, Hillsdale, NJ: Erlbaum.

Alcover, C.-M., Rico, R., Turnley, W. H. and Bolino, M. C. (2017) 'Understanding the changing nature of psychological contracts in 21st century organizations: A multiple-foci exchange relationships approach and proposed framework', *Organizational Psychology Review*, 7, 4-35.

Anderson, J. R. (1983) 'A spreading activation theory of memory', *Journal of Verbal Learning and Verbal Behavior*, 22, 261-295.

Ashford, S. J. and Black, J. S. (1996) 'Proactivity during organizational entry: The role of desire for control', *Journal of Applied Psychology*, 81, 199-214.

Ashford, S. J., Blatt, R. and VandeWalle, D. (2003) 'Reflections on the looking glass: A review of research on feedback-seeking behavior in organizations', *Journal of Management*, 29, 773-799.

Ashford, S. J., Sutcliffe, K. M. and Christianson, M. K. (2009) 'Leadership, voice, and silence', in Greenberg, J. and Edwards, M. S., eds., *Voice and silence in organizations*, Bingley, UK: Emerald Publishing Group, 175-201.

Ashford, S. J., Stobbeleir, K. D. and Nujella, M. (2016) 'To seek or not to seek: Is that the only question? Recent developments in feedback-seeking literature', *Annual Review of Organizational Psychology and Organizational Behavior*, 3, 213-239.

Ashforth, B. E. and Rogers, K. M. (2012) 'Is the employee-organization relationship misspecified?: The centrality of tribes in experiencing the organization', in Shore, L. M., Coyle-Shapiro, J. A.-M. and Tetrick, L. E., eds., *The employee-organization relationship: Applications for the 21st century*, London: Routledge Academic, 22-53.

Ashforth, B. E., Sluss, D. M. and Saks, A. M. (2007) 'Socialization tactics, proactive behavior, and newcomer learning: Integrating socialization models', *Journal of Vocational Behavior*, 70, 447-462.

Bal, P. M., Chiaburu, D. S. and Diaz, I. (2011) 'Does psychological contract breach decrease proactive behaviors? The moderating effect of emotion regulation', *Group & Organization Management*, 36, 722-758.

Baldwin, M. W. and Meunier, J. (1999) 'The cued activation of attachment relational schemas', *Social Cognition*, 17, 209-227.

Baldwin, M. W., Fehr, B., Keedian, E., Seidel, M. and Thomson, D. W. (1993) 'An exploration of the relational schemata underlying attachment styles: Self-report and lexical decision approaches', *Personality and Social Psychology Bulletin*, 19, 746-754.

Baldwin, M. W., Keelan, J. P. R., Fehr, B., Enns, V. and Koh-Rangarajoo, E. (1996) 'Social-cognitive conceptualization of attachment working models: Availability and accessibility effects', *Journal of Personality and Social Psychology*, 71, 94-104.

Bandura, A. (1971) *Social learning theory*, New York, NY: General Learning Press.

Bandura, A. (1994) 'Self-efficacy', in Ramachaudra, V. S., ed., *Encyclopedia of human behaviour*, New York, NY: Academic Press, 71-81.

Bandura, A. (1999) 'A social cognitive theory of personality', in Pervin, L. and John, O., eds., *Handbook of personality*, 2nd edn, New York, NY: Guilford Publications, 154-196.

Bandura, A. (2001) 'Social cognitive theory: An agentic perspective', *Annual Review of Psychology*, 52, 1-26.

Bandura, A. and Locke, E. A. (2003) 'Negative self-efficacy and goal effects revisited', *Journal of Applied Psychology*, 88, 87-99.

Bar-Haim, Y., Sutton, D. B., Fox, N. A. and Marvin, R. S. (2000) 'Stability and change of attachment at 14, 24, and 58 months of age: Behavior, representation, and life events', *Journal of Child Psychology and Psychiatry*, 41, 381-388.

Bartholomew, K. and Horowitz, L. M. (1991) 'Attachment styles among young adults: A test of a four-category model', *Journal of Personality and Social Psychology*, 61, 226-244.

Bass, B. M. (1985) *Leadership and performance beyond expectations*, New York, NY: The Free Press.

Bateman, T. S. and Crant, J. M. (1993) 'The proactive component of organizational behavior: A measure and correlates', *Journal of Organizational Behavior*, 14, 103-118.

Bateman, T. S. and Crant, J. M. (1999) 'Proactive behavior: Meaning, impact, recommendations', *Business Horizons*, 42, 63-70.

Belschak, F. D. and Den Hartog, D. N. (2010) 'Pro-self, pro-social, and pro-organizational foci of proactive behavior: Differential antecedents and consequences', *Journal of Occupational and Organizational Psychology*, 83, 475-498.

Bennett, S., Mohr, J., BrintzenhofeSzoc, K. and Saks, L. V. (2008) 'General and supervision-specific attachment styles: Relations to student perceptions of field supervisors', *Journal of Social Work Education*, 44, 75-94.

Berger, L. (2001) *The relationship between accuracy of self-perception and attachment organization in adolescence*, Unpublished undergraduate thesis, University of Virginia.

Berlyne, D. E. (1960) *Conflict, arousal, and curiosity*, New York, NY: McGraw-Hill.

Bindl, U. K., Parker, S. K., Totterdell, P. and Hagger-Johnson, G. (2012) 'Fuel of the self-starter: How mood relates to proactive goal regulation', *Journal of Applied Psychology*, 97, 134-150.

Binnewies, C., Sonnentag, S. and Mojza, E. J. (2009) 'Daily performance at work: Feeling recovered in the morning as a predictor of day-level job performance', *Journal of Organizational Behavior*, 30, 67-93.

Binnewies, C., Sonnentag, S. and Mojza, E. (2010) 'Recovery during the weekend and fluctuations in weekly job performance: A week-level study examining intra-individual relationships', *Journal of Occupational and Organizational Psychology*, 83, 419-441.

Blau, G. (1994) 'Testing a two dimensional measure of job search behavior', *Organizational Behavior and Human Decision Processes*, 59, 288-312.

Bowlby, J. (1997 [1969]) *Attachment and loss. Vol. 1: Attachment*, London: Pimlico.

Bowlby, J. (1979) *The making and breaking of affectional bonds*, London: Tavistock.

Bowlby, J. (1988) *A secure base*, New York, NY: Basic Books.

Brennan, K. A. and Bosson, J. K. (1998) 'Attachment-style differences in attitudes toward and reactions to feedback from romantic partners: An exploration of the relational bases of self-esteem', *Personality and Social Psychology Bulletin*, 24, 699-714.

Brennan, K. A. and Morris, K. A. (1997) 'Attachment styles, self-esteem, and patterns of seeking feedback from romantic partners', *Personality and Social Psychology Bulletin*, 23, 23-31.

Brennan, K. A., Clark, C. L. and Shaver, P. R. (1998) 'Self-report measurement of adult attachment: An integrative overview', in Simpson, J. A. and Rholes, W. S., eds., *Attachment theory and close relationships*, New York, NY: Guilford Press, 46-76.

Brown, D. J., Cober, R. T., Kane, K., Levy, P. E. and Shalhoop, J. (2006) 'Proactive personality and the successful job search: A field investigation with college graduates', *Journal of Applied Psychology*, 91, 717-726.

Buss, A. H. and Finn, S. E. (1987) 'Classification of personality traits', *Journal of Personality and Social Psychology*, 52, 432-444.

Campbell, D. J. (2000) 'The proactive employee: Managing workplace initiative', *Academy of Management Executive*, 14, 52-66.

Carnelley, K. B. and Rowe, A. C. (2007) 'Repeated priming of attachment security influences later views of self and relationships', *Personal Relationships*, 14, 307-320.

Carver, C. S. and Scheier, M. F. (1982) 'Control theory: A useful conceptual framework for personality-social, clinical, and health psychology', *Psychological Bulletin*, 92, 111-135.

Cassidy, J. (2008) 'The nature of the child's ties', in Cassidy, J. and Shaver, P. R., eds., *Handbook of attachment: Theory, research, and clinical applications*, New York, NY: Guilford Press, 3-20.

Cassidy, J. and Kobak, R. R. (1988) 'Avoidance and its relation to other defensive processes', in Belsky, J. and Nezworski, T., eds., *Clinical implications of attachment*, Hillsdale, NJ: Erlbaum, 300-323.

Cervone, D. and Pervin, L. A. (2008) *Personality: Theory and research*, 10th edn, New York, NY: John Wiley & Sons.

Chen, G. and Kanfer, R. (2006) 'Toward a systems theory of motivated behavior in work teams', *Research in Organizational Behavior*, 27, 223-267.

Choi, J. N. (2007) 'Change-oriented organizational citizenship behavior: Effects of work environment characteristics and intervening psychological processes', *Journal of Organizational Behavior*, 28, 467-484.

Claes, R. and Ruiz-Quintanilla, S. A. (1998) 'Influences of early career experiences, occupational group, and national culture on proactive career behavior', *Journal of Vocational Behavior*, 52, 357-378.

Collins, A. M. and Loftus, E. F. (1975) 'A spreading-activation theory of semantic processing', *Psychological Review*, 82, 407-428.

Collins, N. L. (1996) 'Working models of attachment: Implications for explanation, emotion, and behavior', *Journal of Personality and Social Psychology*, 71, 810-832.

Collins, N. L. and Read, S. J. (1990) 'Adult attachment, working models, and relationship quality in dating couples', *Journal of Personality and Social Psychology*, 58, 644-663.

Collins, N. L. and Read, S. J. (1994) 'Cognitive representations of attachment: The structure and function of working models', in Bartholomew, K. and Perlman, D., eds., *Advances in personal relationships. Vol. 5: Attachment processes in adulthood*, London: Jessica Kingsley, 53-90.

Collins, N. L. and Feeney, B. C. (2000) 'A safe haven: Support-seeking and caregiving processes in intimate relationships', *Journal of Personality and Social Psychology*, 78, 1053-1073.

Collins, N. L. and Allard, L. M. (2002) 'Cognitive representations of attachment: The content and function of working models', in Fletcher, G. J. O. and Clark, M. S., eds., *Blackwell handbook of social psychology: Interpersonal processes*, Oxford: Blackwell, 60-85.

Collins, N. L. and Ford, M. B. (2010) 'Responding to the needs of others: The interplay of the attachment and caregiving systems in adult intimate relationships', *Journal of Social and Personal Relationships*, 27, 235-244.

Coyle-Shapiro, J. A.-M. and Conway, N. (2005) 'Exchange relationships: Examining psychological contracts and perceived organizational support', *Journal of Applied Psychology*, 90, 774-781.

Coyle-Shapiro, J. A.-M. and Shore, L. M. (2007) 'The employee–organization relationship: where do we go from here?', *Human Resource Management Review*, 17, 166-179.

Coyle-Shapiro, J. A.-M. and Parzefall, M.-R. (2008) 'Psychological contracts', in Cooper, C. L. and Barling, J., eds., *The SAGE handbook of organizational behavior*, London, UK: Sage Publications, 17-34.

Cozzarelli, C., Hoekstra, S. J. and Bylsma, W. H. (2000) 'General versus specific mental models of attachment: Are they associated with different outcomes?', *Personality and Social Psychology Bulletin*, 26, 605-618.

Cozzarelli, C., Karafa, J. A., Collins, N. L. and Tagler, M. J. (2003) 'Stability and change in adult attachment styles: Associations with personal vulnerabilities, life events, and global construals of self and others', *Journal of Social and Clinical Psychology*, 22, 315-346.

Crant, J. M. (2000) 'Proactive behavior in organizations', *Journal of Management*, 26, 435-462.

Crant, J. M., Kim, T.-Y. and Wang, J. (2011) 'Dispositional antecedents of demonstration and usefulness of voice behavior', *Journal of Business and Psychology*, 26, 285-297.

Crowell, J. A., Treboux, D. and Waters, E. (2002) 'Stability of attachment representations: The transition to marriage', *Developmental Psychology*, 38, 467-479.

Davidovitz, R., Mikulincer, M., Shaver, P. R., Izsak, R. and Popper, M. (2007) 'Leaders as attachment figures: Leaders' attachment orientations predict leadership-related mental representations and followers' performance and mental health', *Journal of Personality and Social Psychology*, 93, 632-650.

Davila, J. and Cobb, R. J. (2003) 'Predicting change in self-reported and interviewer-assessed adult attachment: Tests of the individual difference and life stress models of attachment change', *Personality and Social Psychology Bulletin*, 29, 859-870.

Davila, J. and Sargent, E. (2003) 'The meaning of life (events) predicts change in attachment security', *Personality and Social Psychology Bulletin*, 29, 1383-1395.

Davila, J., Karney, B. R. and Bradbury, T. N. (1999) 'Attachment change processes in the early years of marriage', *Journal of Personality and Social Psychology*, 76, 783-802.

Davila, J., Burge, D. and Hammen, C. (1997) 'Why does attachment style change?', *Journal of Personality and Social Psychology*, 73, 826-838.

Deci, E. L. and Ryan, R. M. (1985) *Intrinsic motivation and self-determination in human behavior*, New York, NY: Plenum.

Den Hartog, D. N. and Belschak, F. D. (2007) 'Personal initiative, commitment and affect at work', *Journal of Occupational and Organizational Psychology*, 80, 601-622.

Den Hartog, D. N. and Belschak, F. D. (2012) 'When does transformational leadership enhance employee proactive behavior? The role of autonomy and role breadth self-efficacy', *Journal of Applied Psychology*, 97, 194-202.

Detert, J. R. and Burris, E. R. (2007) 'Leadership behavior and employee voice: Is the door really open?', *Academy of Management Journal*, 50, 869-884.

De Vos, A., De Clippeleer, I. and Dewilde, T. (2009) 'Proactive career behaviours and career success during the early career', *Journal of Occupational and Organizational Psychology*, 82, 761–777.

Dozier, M. and Lee, S. W. (1995) 'Discrepancies between self- and other-report of psychiatric symptomatology: Effects of dismissing attachment strategies', *Development and Psychopathology*, 7, 217–226.

Duan, J., Li, C., Xu, Y. and Wu, C.-H. (2017) 'Transformational leadership and employee voice behavior: A Pygmalion mechanism', *Journal of Organizational Behavior*, 38, 650–670.

Dutton, J. E., Ashford, S. J., O'Neill, R. M., Hayes, E. and Wierba, E. E. (1997) 'Reading the wind: How middle managers assess the context for selling issues to top managers', *Strategic Management Journal*, 18, 407–425.

Dykas, M. J. and Cassidy, J. (2011) 'Attachment and the processing of social information across the life span: Theory and evidence', *Psychological Bulletin*, 137, 19–46.

Eccles, J. S. and Wigfield, A. (2002) 'Motivational beliefs, values, and goals', *Annual Review of Psychology*, 53, 109–132.

Edmondson, A. (1999) 'Psychological safety and learning behavior in work teams', *Administrative Science Quarterly*, 44, 350–383.

Edwards, E. P., Eiden, R. D. and Leonard, K. E. (2004) 'Impact of fathers' alcoholism and associated risk factors on parent–infant attachment stability from 12 to 18 months', *Infant Mental Health Journal*, 25, 556–579.

Egeland, B. and Farber, E. A. (1984) 'Infant-mother attachment: Factors related to its development and changes over time', *Child Development*, 55, 753–771.

Eisenberger, R., Huntington, R., Hutchison, S. and Sowa, D. (1986) 'Perceived organizational support', *Journal of Applied Psychology*, 71, 500–507.

Elliot, A. J. and Reis, H. T. (2003) 'Attachment and exploration in adulthood', *Journal of Personality and Social Psychology*, 85, 317–331.

Feeney, B. C. and Collins, N. L. (2001) 'Predictors of caregiving in adult intimate relationships: An attachment theoretical perspective', *Journal of Personality and Social Psychology*, 80, 972–994.

Feeney, B. C. and Thrush, R. L. (2010) 'Relationship influences on exploration in adulthood: The characteristics and function of a secure base', *Journal of Personality and Social Psychology*, 98, 57-76.

Feeney, B. C., Cassidy, J. and Ramos-Marcuse, F. (2008) 'The generalization of attachment representations to new social situations: Predicting behavior during initial interactions with strangers', *Journal of Personality and Social Psychology*, 95, 1481-1498.

Feeney, J. A. and Noller, P. (1990) 'Attachment style as a predictor of adult romantic relationships', *Journal of Personality and Social Psychology*, 58, 281-291.

Fisher, J. D., Nadler, A. and Whitcher-Alagna, S. (1982) 'Recipient reactions to aid', *Psychological Bulletin*, 91, 27-54.

Fleeson, W. (2001) 'Toward a structure- and process-integrated view of personality: Traits as density distributions of states', *Journal of Personality and Social Psychology*, 80, 1011-1027.

Fleeson, W. and Gallagher, P. (2009) 'The implications of Big Five standing for the distribution of trait manifestation in behavior: Fifteen experience-sampling studies and a meta-analysis', *Journal of Personality and Social Psychology*, 97, 1097-1114.

Florian, V., Mikulincer, M. and Ilan, B. (1995) 'Effects of adult attachment style on the perception and search for social support', *Journal of Psychology*, 129, 665-676.

Ford, M. E. (1992) *Motivating humans: Goals, emotions, and personal agency beliefs*, Newbury Park, CA: Sage Publications.

Fraley, R. C. (2002) 'Attachment stability from infancy to adulthood: Meta-analysis and dynamic modeling of developmental mechanisms', *Personality and Social Psychology Review*, 6, 123-151.

Fraley, R. C., Vicary, A. M., Brumbaugh, C. C. and Roisman, G. I. (2011) 'Patterns of stability in adult attachment: An empirical test of two models of continuity and change', *Journal of Personality and Social Psychology*, 101, 974-992.

Fredrickson, B. L. (1998) 'What good are positive emotions?', *Review of General Psychology*, 2, 300-319.

Fredrickson, B. L. (2001) 'The role of positive emotions in positive psychology: The broaden-and-build theory of positive emotions', *American Psychologist*, 56, 218-226.

Frese, M. and Fay, D. (2001) 'Personal initiative (PI): An active performance concept for work in the 21st century', in Staw, B. M. and Sutton, R. M., eds., *Research in organizational behavior*, Amsterdam: Elsevier Science, 133-187.

Frese, M., Garst, H. and Fay, D. (2007) 'Making things happen: Reciprocal relationships between work characteristics and personal initiative in a four-wave longitudinal structural equation model', *Journal of Applied Psychology*, 92, 1084-1102.

Fritz, C. and Sonnentag, S. (2009) 'Antecedents of day-level proactive behavior: A look at job stressors and positive affect during the workday', *Journal of Management*, 35, 94-111.

Fuller, J. B. and Marler, L. E. (2009) 'Change driven by nature: A meta-analytic review of the proactive personality literature', *Journal of Vocational Behavior*, 75, 329-345.

Fuller, J. B., Marler, L. E. and Hester, K. (2006) 'Promoting felt responsibility for constructive change and proactive behavior: Exploring aspects of an elaborated model of work design', *Journal of Organizational Behavior*, 27, 1089-1120.

Game, A. M. (2008) 'Negative emotions in supervisory relationships: The role of relational models', *Human Relations*, 61, 355-393.

Geller, D. and Bamberger, P. (2009) 'Bringing avoidance and anxiety to the job: Attachment style and instrumental helping behavior among co-workers', *Human Relations*, 62, 1803-1827.

Gillath, O., Selcuk, E. and Shaver, P. R. (2008) 'Moving toward a secure attachment style: Can repeated security priming help?', *Social and Personality Psychology Compass*, 2/4, 1651-1666.

Granqvist, P. and Kirkpatrick, L. A. (2008) 'Attachment and religious representations and behavior', in Cassidy, J. and Shaver, P. R., eds., *Handbook of attachment: Theory, research, and clinical applications*, 2nd edn, New York, NY: Guilford Press, 906-933.

Grant, A. M. and Ashford, S. J. (2008) 'The dynamics of proactivity at work', *Research in Organizational Behavior*, 28, 3-34.

Grant, A. M. and Mayer, D. M. (2009) 'Good soldiers and good actors: Prosocial and impression management motives as interactive predictors of affiliative citizenship behaviors', *Journal of Applied Psychology*, 94, 900-912.

Green, J. D. and Campbell, W. K. (2000) 'Attachment and exploration in adults: Chronic and contextual accessibility', *Personality and Social Psychology Bulletin*, 26, 452-461.

Greenleaf, R. K. (1977) *Servant leadership: A journey into the nature of legitimate power and greatness*, New York, NY: Paulist Press.

Griffin, M. A., Neal, A. and Parker, S. K. (2007) 'A new model of work role performance: Positive behavior in uncertain and interdependent contexts', *Academy of Management Journal*, 50, 327-347.

Grossmann, E., Grossmann, K., Heinz, K. and Zimmermann, P. (2008) 'A wider view of attachment and exploration: The influence of mothers and fathers on the development of psychological security from infancy to young adulthood', in Cassidy, J. and Shaver, P. R., eds., *Handbook of attachment: Theory, research, and clinical applications*, 2nd edn, New York, NY: Guilford Press, 857-879.

Gruman, J. A., Saks, A. M. and Zweig, D. I. (2006) 'Organizational socialization tactics and newcomer proactive behaviors: An integrative study', *Journal of Vocational Behavior*, 69, 90-104.

Hakanen, J. J., Perhoniemia, R. and Toppinen-Tanner, S. (2008) 'Positive gain spirals at work: From job resources to work engagement, personal initiative and work-unit innovativeness', *Journal of Vocational Behavior*, 73, 78-91.

Hammond, J. R. and Fletcher, G. J. O. (1991) 'Attachment styles and relationship satisfaction in the development of close relationships', *New Zealand Journal of Psychology*, 20, 56-62.

Hazan, C. and Shaver, P. R. (1987) 'Romantic love conceptualized as an attachment process', *Journal of Personality and Social Psychology*, 52, 511-524.

Hebb, D. O. (1955) 'Drives and the C. N. S. (conceptual nervous system)', *Psychological Review*, 62, 243-254.

Hepper, E. G. and Carnelley, K. B. (2010) 'Adult attachment and feedback-seeking patterns in relationships and work', *European Journal of Social Psychology*, 40, 448-464.

Hollenbeck, J. R. and Williams, C. R. (1987) 'Goal importance, self-focus, and the goal-setting process', *Journal of Applied Psychology*, 72, 204-211.

Hui, C., Lee, C. and Rousseau, D. M. (2004) 'Psychological contract and organizational citizenship behavior in China: Investigating generalizability and instrumentality', *Journal of Applied Psychology*, 89, 311-321.

Hunt, J. M. V. (1963) 'Motivation inherent in information processing and action', in Harvey, O. J., ed., *Motivation and social interaction: Cognitive determinants*, New York, NY: Ronald, 35-94.

Isen, A. M. (1999) 'On the relationship between affect and creative problem solving', in Russ, S., ed., *Affect, creative experience, and psychological adjustment*, Philadelphia, PA: Taylor & Francis, 3-17.

Janssen, O. (2000) 'Job demands, perceptions of effort-reward fairness and innovative work behaviour', *Journal of Occupational and Organizational Psychology*, 73, 287-302.

John, O. P., Naumann, L. P. and Soto, C. J. (2008) 'Paradigm shift to the integrative Big Five trait taxonomy: History, measurement, and conceptual issues', in Pervin, L. and John, O. P., eds., *Handbook of personality: Theory and research*, 3rd edn, New York, NY: Guilford Press, 114-158.

Kanter, R. M. (1988) 'When a thousand flowers bloom: Structural, collective and social conditions for innovation in organization', in Staw, B. and Cummings, L. L., eds., *Research in organizational behavior*, Greenwich, CT: JAI Press, 169-211.

Keller, T. (2003) 'Parental images as a guide to leadership sensemaking: An attachment perspective on implicit leadership theories', *Leadership Quarterly*, 14, 141-160.

Kirkpatrick, L. A. (1995) 'Attachment theory and religious experience', in Hood, R. W. J., ed., *Handbook of religious experience*, Birmingham, AL: Religious Education Press, 446-475.

Kirkpatrick, L. A. and Hazan, C. (1994) 'Attachment styles and close relationships: A four-year prospective study', *Personal Relationships*, 1, 123-142.

Klein, H. J. (1989) 'An integrated control theory model of work motivation', *Academy of Management Review*, 14, 150-172.

Kobak, R. R. and Sceery, A. (1988) 'Attachment in late adolescence: Working models, affect regulation, and representations of self and others', *Child Development*, 59, 135-146.

Laghi, F., D'Alessio, M., Pallini, S. and Baiocco, R. (2009) 'Attachment representation and time perspective in adolescence', *Social Indicators Research*, 90, 181-194.

Lam, W., Huang, X. and Snape, E. (2007) 'Feedback-seeking behavior and leader-member exchange: Do supervisor-attributed motives matter?', *Academy of Management Journal*, 50, 348-363.

Leary, M. R. (1999) 'Making sense of self-esteem', *Current Directions in Psychological Science*, 8, 32-35.

LePine, J. A. and Van Dyne, L. (1998) 'Predicting voice behavior in work groups', *Journal of Applied Psychology*, 83, 853-868.

LePine, J. A. and Van Dyne, L. (2001) 'Voice and cooperative behavior as contrasting forms of contextual performance: Evidence of differential relationships with big five personality characteristics and cognitive ability', *Journal of Applied Psychology*, 86, 326-336.

Lewis, M., Feiring, C. and Rosenthal, S. (2000) 'Attachment over time', *Child Development*, 71, 707-720.

Locke, E. A. and Latham, G. P. (1990) *A theory of goal setting and task performance*, Englewood Cliffs, NJ: Prentice Hall.

Loewenstein, G. (1994) 'The psychology of curiosity: A review and reinterpretation', *Psychological Bulletin*, 116, 75-98.

Lopez, F. G., Mitchell, P. and Gormley, B. (2002) 'Adult attachment orientations and college student distress: Test of a mediational model', *Journal of Counseling Psychology*, 49, 460-467.

Luke, M. A., Sedikides, C. and Carnelley, K. (2012) 'Your love lifts me higher! The energizing quality of secure relationships', *Personality and Social Psychology Bulletin*, 38, 721-733.

Madjar, N., Oldham, G. R. and Pratt, M. G. (2002) 'There's no place like home? The contributions of work and non-work creativity to support employee's creative performance', *Academy of Management Journal*, 45, 757-767

Madrid, H. P., Patterson, M. G., Birdi, K. S., Leiva, P. I. and Kausel, E. E. (2014) 'The role of weekly high-activated positive mood, context, and personality in innovative work behavior: A multilevel and interactional model', *Journal of Organizational Behavior*, 35, 234-256.

Main, M. (1981) 'Avoidance in the service of attachment: A working paper', in Immelman, K., Barlow, G., Petrinovitch, L. and Main, M., eds., *Behavioral development: The Bielefeld interdisciplinary project*, New York, NY: Cambridge University Press, 651-693.

Main, M. (1990) 'Cross-cultural studies of attachment organization: Recent studies, changing methodologies, and the concept of conditional strategies', *Human Development*, 33, 48-61.

Major, D. A., Turner, J. E. and Fletcher, T. D. (2006) 'Linking proactive personality and the Big Five to motivation to learn and development activity', *Journal of Applied Psychology*, 91, 927-935.

Mallinckrodt, B. and Wei, M. (2005) 'Attachment, social competencies, social support, and psychological distress', *Journal of Counseling Psychology*, 52, 358-367.

Maynes, T. D. and Podsakoff, P. M. (2014) 'Speaking more broadly: An examination of the nature, antecedents, and consequences of an expanded set of employee voice behaviors', *Journal of Applied Psychology*, 99, 87-112.

Mayseless, O. and Popper, M. (2007) 'Reliance on leaders and social institutions: An attachment perspective', *Attachment and Human Development*, 9, 73-93.

Mikulincer, M. (1995) 'Attachment style and the mental representation of the self', *Journal of Personality and Social Psychology*, 69, 1203-1215.

Mikulincer, M. (1997) 'Adult attachment style and information processing: Individual differences in curiosity and cognitive closure', *Journal of Personality and Social Psychology*, 72, 1217-1230.

Mikulincer, M. (1998) 'Attachment working models and the sense of trust: An exploration of interaction goals and affect regulation', *Journal of Personality and Social Psychology*, 74, 1209-1224.

Mikulincer, M. and Florian, V. (1995) 'Appraisal of and coping with a real-life stressful situation: The contribution of attachment styles', *Personality and Social Psychology Bulletin*, 21, 406-414.

Mikulincer, M. and Orbach, I. (1995) 'Attachment styles and repressive defensiveness: The accessibility and architecture of affective memories', *Journal of Personality and Social Psychology*, 68, 917-925.

Mikulincer, M. and Shaver, P. R. (2001) 'Attachment theory and intergroup bias: Evidence that priming the secure base schema attenuates negative reactions to out-groups', *Journal of Personality and Social Psychology*, 81, 97-115

Mikulincer, M. and Shaver, P. R. (2003) 'The attachment behavioral system in adulthood: Activation, psychodynamics, and interpersonal processes', in Zanna, M. P., ed., *Advances in experimental social psychology*, New York, NY: Academic Press, 53-152.

Mikulincer, M. and Shaver, P. R. (2005) 'Attachment security, compassion, and altruism', *Current Directions in Psychological Science*, 14, 34-38.

Mikulincer, M. and Shaver, P. R. (2007a) *Attachment in adulthood: Structure, dynamics, and change*, New York, NY: Guilford Press.

Mikulincer, M. and Shaver, P. R. (2007b) 'Boosting attachment security to promote mental health, prosocial values, and inter-group tolerance', *Psychological Inquiry*, 18, 139-156.

Mikulincer, M. and Shaver, P. R. (2012) 'Attachment theory expanded: A behavioral systems approach to personality', in Deaux, K. and Snyder, M., eds., *Oxford handbook of personality and social psychology*, New York, NY: Oxford University Press, 467-492.

Mikulincer, M., Gillatha, O. and Shaver, P. R. (2002) 'Activation of the attachment system in adulthood: Threat-related primes increase the accessibility of mental representations of attachment figures', *Journal of Personality and Social Psychology*, 83, 881-895.

Mikulincer, M., Shaver, P. R. and Horesh, N. (2006) 'Attachment bases of emotion regulation and posttraumatic adjustment', in Snyder, D. K., Simpson, J. A. and Hughes, J. N., eds., *Emotion regulation in families: Pathways to dysfunction and health*, Washington, DC: American Psychological Association, 77-99.

Mikulincer, M., Hirschberger, G., Nachmias, O. and Gillath, O. (2001) 'The affective component of the secure base schema: Affective priming with representations of attachment security', *Journal of Personality and Social Psychology*, 80, 305-321.

Mikulincer, M., Shaver, P. R., Gillath, O. and Nitzberg, R. A. (2005) 'Attachment, caregiving, and altruism: Boosting attachment security increases compassion and helping', *Journal of Personality and Social Psychology*, 89, 817-839.

Miller, G. A., Galanter, E. and Pribram, K. H. (1960) *Plans and the structure of behavior*, New York, NY: Holt.

Minbashian, A., Wood, R. E. and Beckmann, N. (2010) 'Task-contingent conscientiousness as a unit of personality at work', *Journal of Applied Psychology*, 95, 793-806.

Mischel, W. and Shoda, Y. (1995) 'A cognitive-affective system theory of personality: Reconceptualizing situations, dispositions, dynamics, and invariance in personality structure', *Psychological Review*, 102, 246-268.

Morrison, E. W. and Bies, R. J. (1991) 'Impression management in the feedback-seeking process: A literature review and research agenda', *Academy of Management Review*, 16, 522-541.

Morrison, E. W. and Phelps, C. C. (1999) 'Taking charge at work: Extrarole efforts to initiate workplace change', *Academy of Management Journal*, 42, 403-419.

Neustadt, E., Chamorro-Premuzic, T. and Furnham, A. (2006) 'The relationship between personality traits, self-esteem, and attachment at work', *Journal of Individual Differences*, 27, 208-217.

Ognibene, T. C. and Collins, N. L. (1998) 'Adult attachment styles, perceived social support and coping strategies', *Journal of Social and Personal Relationships*, 15, 323-345.

Overall, N. C., Fletcher, G. J. O. and Friesen, M. D. (2003) 'Mapping the intimate relationship mind: Comparisons between three models of attachment representations', *Personality and Social Psychology Bulletin*, 29, 1479-1493.

Owens, B. P., Baker, W. E., Sumpter, D. M. and Cameron, K. S. (2016) 'Relational energy at work: Implications for job engagement and job performance', *Journal of Applied Psychology*, 101, 35-49.

Panaccio, A., Henderson, D. J., Liden, R. C., Wayne, S. J. and Cao, X. (2015) 'Toward an understanding of when and why servant leadership accounts for employee extra-role behaviors', *Journal of Business and Psychology*, 30, 657-675.

Park, L. E., Crocker, J. and Mickelson, K. D. (2004) 'Attachment styles and contingencies of self-worth', *Personality and Social Psychology Bulletin*, 30, 1243-1254.

Parker, S. K. and Collins, C. G. (2010) 'Taking stock: Integrating and differentiating multiple proactive behaviors', *Journal of Management*, 36, 633-662.

Parker, S. K. and Bindl, U. K., eds. (2017) *Proactivity at work*, New York, NY: Routledge.

Parker, S. K., Wall, T. D. and Jackson, P. R. (1997) '"That's not my job": Developing flexible employee work orientations', *Academy of Management Journal*, 40 899-929.

Parker, S. K., Williams, H. M. and Turner, N. (2006) 'Modeling the antecedents of proactive behavior at work', *Journal of Applied Psychology*, 91, 636-652.

Parker, S. K., Bindl, U. K. and Strauss, K. (2010) 'Making things happen: A model of proactive motivation', *Journal of Management*, 36, 827-856.

Piaget, J. (1953) *Logic and psychology*, Manchester: Manchester University Press.

Piaget, J. (1969) *Psychology of intelligence*, Totowa, NJ: Littlefield, Adams.

Pierce, T. and Lydon, J. E. (2001) 'Global and specific relational models in the experience of social interactions', *Journal of Personality and Social Psychology*, 80, 613-631.

Podsakoff, P. M., MacKenzie, S. B., Paine, J. B. and Bachrach, D. G. (2000) 'Organizational citizenship behaviors: A critical review of the theoretical and empirical literature and suggestions for future research', *Journal of Management*, 26, 513-563.

Popper, M. (2002) 'Narcissism and attachment patterns of personalized and socialized charismatic leaders', *Journal of Social and Personal Relationships*, 19, 797-809.

Popper, M. and Mayseless, O. (2003) 'Back to basics: Applying a parenting perspective to transformational leadership', *Leadership Quarterly*, 14, 41-65.

Popper, M., Mayseless, O. and Castelnovo, O. (2000) 'Transformational leadership and attachment', *Leadership Quarterly*, 11, 267-289.

Popper, M., Amit, K., Gal, R., Mishkal-Sinai, M. and Lisak, A. (2004) 'The capacity to lead: Major psychological differences between leaders and nonleaders', *Military Psychology*, 16, 245-263.

Raabe, B., Frese, M. and Beehr, T. A. (2007) 'Action regulation theory and career self-management', *Journal of Vocational Behavior*, 70, 297-311.

Rank, J., Carsten, J. M., Unger, J. M. and Spector, P. E. (2007) 'Proactive customer service performance: Relationships with individual, task, and leadership variables', *Human Performance*, 20, 363-390.

Raub, S. and Liao, H. (2012) 'Doing the right thing without being told: Joint effects of initiative climate and general self-efficacy on employee proactive customer service performance', *Journal of Applied Psychology*, 97, 651-667.

Rhoades, L. and Eisenberger, R. (2002) 'Perceived organizational support: A review of the literature', *Journal of Applied Psychology*, 87, 698-714.

Richards, D. A. and Schat, A. C. (2011) 'Attachment at (not to) work: Applying attachment theory to explain individual behavior in organizations', *Journal of Applied Psychology*, 96, 169-182.

Richards, D. A. and Hackett, R. D. (2012) 'Attachment and emotion regulation: Compensatory interactions and leader–member exchange', *Leadership Quarterly*, 23, 686-701.

Rioux, S. M. and Penner, L. A. (2001) 'The causes of organizational citizenship behavior: A motivational analysis', *Journal of Applied Psychology*, 86, 1306-1314.

Roberts, J. E., Gotlib, I. H. and Kassel, J. D. (1996) 'Adult attachment security and symptoms of depression: The mediating roles of dysfunctional attitudes and low self-esteem', *Journal of Personality and Social Psychology*, 70, 310-320.

Robinson, S. L. and Bennett, R. J. (1995) 'A typology of deviant workplace behaviors: A multidimensional scaling study', *Academy of Management Journal*, 38, 555-572.

Robinson, S. L., Kraatz, M. S. and Rousseau, D. M. (1994) 'Changing obligations and the pscyhological contract: a longitudinal study', *Academy of Management Journal*, 37, 137-151.

Rotundo, M. and Sackett, P. R. (2002) 'The relative importance of task, citizenship, and counterproductive performance to global ratings of job performance: A policy-capturing approach', *Journal of Applied Psychology*, 87, 66-80.

Rousseau, D. M. (1989) 'Psychological and implied contracts in organizations', *Employee Responsibilities and Rights Journal*, 2, 121-139.

Rousseau, D. M. (1995) *Psychological contracts in organizations: Understanding written and unwritten agreements*, Newbury Park, CA: Sage Publications.

Rousseau, D. M. and Wade-Benzoni, K. A. (1994) 'Linking strategy and human resource practices: How employee and customer contracts are created', *Human Resource Management*, 33, 463-489.

Ruvolo, A. P., Fabin, L. A. and Ruvolo, C. M. (2001) 'Relationship experiences and change in attachment characteristics of young adults: The role of relationship breakups and conflict avoidance', *Personal Relationships*, 8, 265-281.

Ryan, R. M. and Frederick, C. (1997) 'On energy, personality, and health: Subjective vitality as a dynamic reflection of wellbeing', *Journal of Personality*, 65, 529-565.

Ryan, R. M. and Deci, E. L. (2000) 'Self-determination theory and the facilitation of intrinsic motivation, social development, and well-being', *American Psychologist*, 55, 68-78.

Sackett, P. R., Berry, C. M., Wiemann, S. A. and Laczo, R. M. (2006) 'Citizenship and counterproductive behavior: Clarifying relations between the two domains', *Human Performance*, 19, 441-464.

Sagi-Schwartz, A. and Aviezer, O. (2005) 'Correlates of attachment to multiple caregivers in kibbutz children from birth to emerging adulthood: The Haifa longitudinal study', in Grossmann, K. E., Grossmann, K. and Waters, E., eds., *Attachment from infancy to adulthood*, New York, NY: Guilford Press, 165-197.

Salanova, M. and Schaufeli, W. B. (2008) 'A cross-national study of work engagement as a mediator between job resources and proactive behaviour', *International Journal of Human Resource Management*, 19, 116-131.

Scharfe, E. and Bartholomew, K. (1994) 'Reliability and stability of adult attachment patterns', *Personal Relationships*, 23-43.

Schaufeli, W. B., Salanova, M., González-romá, V. and Bakker, A. B. (2002) 'The measurement of engagement and burnout: A two sample confirmatory factor analytic approach', *Journal of Happiness Studies*, 3, 71-92.

Schirmer, L. L. and Lopez, F. G. (2001) 'Probing the social support and work strain relationship among adult workers: Contributions of adult attachment orientations', *Journal of Vocational Behavior*, 59, 17-33.

Scott, S. G. and Bruce, R. A. (1994) 'Determinants of innovative behavior: A path model of individual innovation in the workplace', *Academy of Management Journal*, 37, 580-607.

Seo, M.-G., Bartunek, J. M. and Barrett, L. F. (2004) 'The role of affective experience in work motivation', *Academy of Management Review*, 29, 423-439.

Shaver, P. R., Schachner, D. A. and Mikulincer, M. (2005) 'Attachment style, excessive reassurance seeking, relationship processes, and depression', *Personality and Social Psychology Bulletin*, 31, 1-17.

Shaver, P. R., Segev, M. and Mikulincer, M. (2011) 'A behavioral systems perspective on power and aggression', in Shaver, P. R. and Mikulincer, M., eds., *Human aggression and violence: Causes, manifestations, and consequences*, Washington, DC: American Psychological Association, 71-87.

Sheldon, K. M. and Elliot, A. J. (1999) 'Goal striving, need-satisfaction, and longitudinal well-being: The self-concordance model', *Journal of Personality and Social Psychology*, 76, 482-497.

Sibley, C. G. and Overall, N. C. (2008) 'Modeling the hierarchical structure of attachment representations: A test of domain differentiation', *Personality and Individual Differences*, 44, 238-249.

Simpson, J. A., Rholes, W. S., Campbell, L. and Wilson, C. L. (2003) 'Changes in attachment orientations across the transition to parenthood', *Journal of Experimental Social Psychology*, 39, 317-331.

Smith, E. R., Murphy, J. and Coats, S. (1999) 'Attachment to groups: Theory and measurement', *Journal of Personality and Social Psychology*, 77, 94-110.

Sonnentag, S. (2003) 'Recovery, work engagement, and proactive behavior: A new look at the interface between nonwork and work', *Journal of Applied Psychology*, 88, 518-528.

Srivastava, S. and Beer, J. S. (2005) 'How self-evaluations relate to being liked by others: Integrating sociometer and attachment perspectives', *Journal of Personality and Social Psychology*, 89, 966-977.

Thomas, J. P., Whitman, D. S. and Viswesvaran, C. (2010) 'Employee proactivity in organizations: A comparative meta-analysis of emergent proactive constructs', *Journal of Occupational and Organizational Psychology*, 83, 275-300.

Thompson, J. A. (2005) 'Proactive personality and job performance: A social capital perspective', *Journal of Applied Psychology*, 90, 1011-1017.

Tidwell, M. and Sias, P. (2005) 'Personality and information seeking: Understanding how traits influence information-seeking behaviors', *Journal of Business Communication*, 42, 51-77.

Tinbergen, N. (1951) *The study of instinct*, Oxford: Clarendon Press.

Tsagarakis, M., Kafetsios, K. and Stalikas, A. (2007) 'Reliability and validity of the Greek version of the Revised Experiences in Close Relationships measure of adult attachment', *European Journal of Psychological Assessment*, 23, 47-55.

Tsai, W.-C., Chen, C.-C. and Liu, H.-L. (2007) 'Test of a model linking employee positive moods and task performance', *Journal of Applied Psychology*, 92, 1570-1583.

Van Dyne, L. and Le Pine, J. A. (1998) 'Helping and voice extra-role behaviors: Evidence of construct and predictive validity', *Academy of Management Journal*, 41, 108-119.

Vaughn, B., Egeland, B., Sroufe, L. A. and Waters, E. (1979) 'Individual differences in infant-mother attachment at twelve and eighteen months: Stability and change in families under stress', *Child Development*, 50, 971-975.

Vondra, J. I., Hommerding, K. D. and Shaw, D. S. (1999) 'Stability and change in infant attachment in a low-income sample', *Monographs of the Society for Research in Child Development*, 64, 119-144.

Von Krogh, G. (1998) 'Care in knowledge creation', *California Management Review*, 40, 133-153.

Vroom, V. H. (1964) *Work and motivation*, New York, NY: John Wiley & Sons.

Wall, T. D., Cordery, J. L. and Clegg, C. W. (2002) 'Empowerment, performance and operational uncertainty: A theoretical integration', *Applied Psychology. An International Review*, 51, 146-169.

Wallin, D. J. (2007) *Attachment in psychotherapy*, New York, NY: Guilford Press.

Walumbwa, F. O. and Schaubroeck, J. (2009) 'Leader personality traits and employee voice behavior: Mediating roles of ethical leadership and work group psychological safety', *Journal of Applied Psychology*, 94, 1275-1286.

Wang, Y., Ang, C., Jiang, Z. and Wu, C.-H. (2018) 'The role of trait extraversion in shaping proactive behavior: A multilevel examination of the impact of high-activated positive affect', *Personality and Individual Differences*, 136, 107-112.

Wang, Y., Wu, C.-H., Parker, S. K. and Griffin, M. A. (2018) 'Developing goal orientations conducive to learning and performance: An intervention study', *Journal of Occupational and Organizational Psychology*, 91, 875-895.

Waters, E., Merrick, S., Treboux, D., Crowell, J. and Albersheim, L. (2000) 'Attachment security in infancy and early adulthood: A twenty-year longitudinal study', *Child Development*, 71, 684-689.

Wei, M. and Ku, T.-Y. (2007) 'Testing a conceptual model of working through self-defeating patterns', *Journal of Counseling Psychology*, 54, 295-305.

Wei, M., Heppner, P. P. and Mallinckrodt, B. (2003) 'Perceived coping as a mediator between attachment and psychological distress: A structural equation modeling approach', *Journal of Counseling Psychology*, 50, 438-447.

Weiss, R. S. (1998) 'A taxonomy of relationships', *Journal of Social and Personal Relationships*, 15, 671-683

West, M. A. and Richter, A. W. (2011) 'Team climate and effectiveness outcomes', in Ashkanasy, N., Wilderom, C. P. M. and Peterson, M. F., eds., *Handbook of organizational culture and climate*, London: Sage Publications, 249-270.

Westen, D., Gabbard, G. O. and Ortigo, K. M. (2008) 'Psychoanalytic approaches to personality', in John, O. P., Robins, R. W. and Pervin, L. A., eds., *Handbook of personality: Theory and research*, 3rd edn, New York, NY: Guilford Press, *61*-113.

White, R. W. (1959) 'Motivation reconsidered: The concept of competence', *Psychological Review*, 66, 279-333.

Wrzesniewski, A. and Dutton, J. E. (2001) 'Crafting a job: Revisioning employees as active crafters of their work', *Academy of Management Review*, 26, 179-201.

Wu, C.-H. (2009) 'The relationship between attachment style and self-concept clarity: The mediation effect of self-esteem', *Personality and Individual Differences*, 47, 42-46.

Wu, C.-H. and Yao, G. (2008) 'Psychometric analysis of the short-form UCLA Loneliness Scale (ULS-8) in Taiwanese undergraduate students', *Personality and Individual Differences*, 44, 1762-1771.

Wu, C.-H. and Parker, S. K. (2012) 'The role of attachment styles in shaping proactive behaviour: An intra-individual analysis', *Journal of Occupational and Organizational Psychology*, 85, 523-530.

Wu, C.-H. and Wang, Z. (2015) 'How transformational leadership shapes team proactivity: The mediating role of positive affective tone and the moderating role of team task variety', *Group Dynamics: Theory, Research, and Practice,* 19, 137-151.

Wu, C.-H. and Parker, S. K. (2017) 'The role of leader support in facilitating proactive work behaviour: An perspective from attachment theory', *Journal of Management*, 43, 1025-1049.

Wu, C.-H., Parker, S. K. and Bindl, U. K. (2013) 'Who is proactive and why? Unpacking individual differences in employee proactivity', in Bakker, A. B., ed., *Advances in positive organizational psychology*, Bingley: Emerald Group Publishing, 261-280.

Wu, C.-H., Parker, S. K. and de Jong, J. P. J. (2014) 'Feedback seeking from peers: A positive strategy for insecurely attached team workers', *Human Relations*, 67, 441-464.

Wu, C.-H., Parker, S. K., Wu, L.-Z. and Lee, C. (2018) 'When and why people engage in different forms of proactive behavior: Interactive effects of self-construals and work characteristics', *Academy of Management Journal*, 61, 293-323.

Yusuf, C. (2017) 'The mediating effect of LMX in the relationship between school bureaucratic structure and teachers' proactive behavior', *Leadership & Organization Development Journal*, 38, 780-793.

Zárraga, C. and Bonache, J. (2005) 'The impact of team atmosphere on knowledge outcomes in self-managed teams', *Organization Studies*, 26, 661-681.

Index

A

action 9
affective traits 88, 89
affiliation behavioural system 29, 30, *31*, 102
Ainsworth et al. 33–4
ambivalent attachment 34, 35, 69, 69–70
anthropomorphization 78
anxious attachment 38, 39
  and intimacy 41
  negative model of others 39
  response to negative attachment-relevant events 41
Ashforth, B.E. and Rogers, K.M. 78
assertiveness 88
attachment anxiety 35, 70, 72, 94, 97, 98, 101–2
  caregivers 96
  and leader secure-based support 74
  support seeking 101
attachment avoidance 35, 70, 72, 94, 97, 98, 101
  and leader secure-based support 75
  support seekers 96
attachment behavioural system 23–4, 25, 29, 30, *31*, 32–7, 101, 102
  attachment anxiety 35
  attachment avoidance 35
  and attachment figures 32–3
  characteristics of infants and caregivers 33
  deactivating strategy 34–5
  development of 32
  hyperactivating strategy 34
  patterns of attachment 33
  purpose of 32
  attachment experiences 36, 37
  context-specific 44–7
attachment figures 37
  availability, sensitivity and responsiveness of 49–50
  outside of families 44–7
  primary 13, 14, 16, 17, 24
    characteristics of 33
    patterns of attachment 33
  proximity to 25, 29, 32, 34, 41
  secondary 43, 46
  subordinate 44
attachment-related memories 37, 38
attachment security 63–5, *64*, 71–2, 83, 93
  higher 94
  research 93
attachment styles 24, 32, 33, 37, 93
  ambivalent attachment 34, 35, 69
  avoidant attachment *see* avoidant attachment
  changeability of 43
  context-specific versus prototype 44–5
  correlation with proactive personality *71*
  in different social contexts 44–7
  and effective relationships 95–7
  secure attachment *see* secure attachment
  stability and changeability of 47–53, 47–54
    changes in the maternal environment 48–9
    disorganized attachment 50
    experimental manipulations 48–50, 50–3
      relational schemas 51, 53, 54
      security-attachment related experiences 51–2
      security priming 50, 51–3
    life events 49
      inconsistent findings 50
    romantic relationships 49–50
    studies 47–8
      childhood 48–9
      longitudinal 48–50
  unstructured/disorganized 35
attachment theory 14–16, 23–4, 43, 85

application to work behaviour
99–103
attachment behavioural system *see*
attachment behavioural system
behavioural systems 23, 24–32
comparison with psychoanalytic
paradigm 16–18
context-specific attachment
experiences 44–7
definition 14
differences from social exchange
approach 85–6
different conceptualizations and
motivational mechanisms of 90–1
and early life experiences 16–17
ethological and evolutionary
element 17
internal working models 24, 27–8,
36–42
and process view of personality
89–90
and secure-based support 93–4
see also attachment figures;
attachment styles
autonomous motivation 10, 64–5, 69
availability 73
avoidant attachment 34, 35, 38, 69,
70
and autonomy 41
negative model of others 39
response to negative attachment-
relevant events 41

B

balanced psychological contracts 80,
81
Bateman, T.S. and Crant, J.M. 3
behaviour
goal-corrected and hierarchical 27
structure 27
behavioural perspective 4–7
behavioural system model of
proactivity 55, 58–62
discrepancy production 59
discrepancy reduction 59
flexibility of 61
goal expectancy 59–60
goal importance 59, 60
goals 58–9
innovation 61

integration of proactivity literature
62, *62*
job crafting 61
link with attachment security 63–5
regulatory energy 59, 60
research 91–2
voice 61
behavioural systems 23, 24–32
activation and termination 25–6,
30
affiliation behavioural system 29,
30, *31*
attachment behavioural system *see*
attachment behavioural system
caregiving behavioural system 29,
30, *31*
causal factors 26–7
chain structure 26
definition 25
development of 28
exploration behavioural system 29,
30, *31*
and instinctive behaviours 24–5
plan hierarchy structure 27, 28
power behavioural system 29–30,
30, *31*
set goals 25
sexual behavioural system 29, 30,
31
sophistication of 28
triggers 28, 30, *31*
variety and complexity of 28–9
between-individual level 91–2
big-five personality framework 84–5,
87–8
Bowlby, John 15, 16, 17, 18, 43, 47
and attachment experiences 37
behavioural systems 23, 24–32
on differing attachment styles 44
goal-corrected behavioural system
99, 100–1, 102–3
internal working models 37
secure base 73
see also attachment behavioural
system; attachment theory; internal
working models

C

can do pathway 8, 9, 14
careers 1–2, 4

goal commitment and information 8
caregiving behavioural system 29, 30, *31*, 101
caregiving process 95–6
Carnelley, K.B. and Rowe, A.C. 52
change-oriented proactive behaviour 5
citizenship behaviour 100
citizenship performance 99
cognitive appraisals 26, 30
cognitive tasks 38
cognitive traits 88–9
Collins, N.L. and Feeney, B.C. 95–6
commitment 10
compensation hypothesis 46–7
compulsive caregiving 94
conflict behaviour 41
context-specific attachment experiences 44–7
context-specific relational models 45
control appraisals 9
control, desire for 10
controlling caregiving 94
counter-productive work behaviour (CWB) 99, 100

D

De Vos et al. 8
deactivating strategy 34–5
discrepancy 58–9
discrepancy-reduction loop 59
disorganized attachment 50
distancing coping strategies 41

E

early life experiences 16–17
Eisenberger et al. 79
emotion-focused strategies 41
employee proactivity 1–3
  careers 1–2, 4, 8
  conceptualizations of 1–2
    behavioural perspective 4–7
    individual differences perspective 3–4
    process perspective 7–8
  creativity and ideas 1
  different conceptualizations and motivational mechanisms of 90–1

dispositional foundation of 86–90
as a form of exploration 55–8
individual differences in 67–71
motivational mechanisms 8
  can do pathway 8, 9, 14
  energized to pathway 8, 11–12, 14
  reason to pathway 8, 9–10, 14
relational basis of 13–18, 84–6
  social exchange perspective 85
relational experiences 13
research 83, 91–8
situational impact on 71–81
  leadership factors 73–7
  organizational factors 78–81
  work team factors 77–8
enacting 8
encouragement of growth 73
energized to pathway 11–12, 14, 65
energy 65, 69
environment, mastering and controlling 56–7, *58*
envisioning 8
evolutionary adaptiveness 17, 18, 23, 29
expectancy theory 59
exploration 55
  concept of 55–6
  and employee proactivity 55–8
  external stimuli 56
  and motivation 56
  reducing knowledge gaps 56
  similarities with proactive behaviour *58*
exploration behavioural system 24, 29, 30, *31*

F

feedback 1–2, 38
Feeney, B.C. and Thrush, R.L. 96–7
felt recovery 11, 12
functional classification of personality 88–9
future-focused proactive behaviour 5
future orientation 68

G

Gillath, O. and Shaver, P.R. 53
global relational models 45–6

goal attainment 64
goal-corrected behavioural system
    99, 100–1, 102–3
goal envisioning 11, 63, 68
goal expectancy 59–60, *62*, 64
goal generation 7, 8
goal importance 59, 60, *62*
goal process 7
goal regulation 60, *62*, *64*
goal striving 7, 8, 11, 59
goals 58–9
Greenleaf, R.K. 76
Griffin et al. 6, 56–7
group-related constructs 46
group-specific attachment styles 46

H

helping behaviour 100, 101–2
high care team atmosphere 77, 78
hyperactivating strategy 34

I

idiosyncratic performances 24–5
individual differences perspective 3–4
information-seeking behaviour 9
initiative 10, 12
innovation 61
insecure attachment 33, 38, 38–9
    and leader secure-based support
        74–5
    negative model of others 39
instinctive behaviours 24–5, 26
instrumental traits 88, 89
internal working models 17, 18, 24,
    27–8, 36–42
    changeable and revisable 28
    function of 27
    goals and strategies in social
        interaction 40–1
    of individuals 36–7
    individuals' expectations of
        relationships 40
    influence of 38–9
    stability of 37
internalized motivation 10
interpersonal relationships 17

J

job crafting 61

job searches 1

L

leader-follower relationships 95–6, 97
leader–member exchange (LMX) 98
leader secure-based support 73–5,
    79, 96–7
leadership 73–7, 76
    attachment-caregiving association
        94
    future research 93
    leader-follower relationships 95–6,
        97
    secure-base support 93–4
life events 49, 50
lower-level goals 27

M

maternal environment 48–9
mental representations 16–17, 36
Mikulincer, M. and Shaver, P.R. 47,
    48
model of the environment 27, 30
model of the self 27, 30
motivation 8
    can do pathway 8, 9, 14
    energized to pathway 8, 11–12, 14
    and exploration 56
    reason to pathway 8, 9–10, 14

N

natural selection 29
negative attachment-related memories
    38
negative self-concept 38–9
neuroticism 88
noninterference 73

O

object relations theories 17
openness to experience 88
organizational citizenship behaviour
    (OCB) 99, 100
organizations 72
    anthropomorphization of 78
    challenges 1
    employee proactivity in 78–81
    research 98–9

P

Parker et al. 8, 9, 11, 13
Parker, S.K. and Collins, C.G. 6
perceived organization support 79
performance recognition 79
personal achievements 41
personal initiative 12, 57
personality 14, 89–90
　functional classification of 88–9
　process view of 87, 89
　structure view of 87
　traits 88–9
　two-level approach 91–3
personality development
　behavioural systems 17, 18
　and early life experiences 16–17
planning 8
Podsakoff et al. 100
positive affect 11–12
positive attachment-related memories
　38
positive self-concept 38, 39, 68
positive self-views 63–4, 68, 69
power behavioural system 29–30, 30,
　31, 102
primary goals 27
proactive behaviour 1–2, 55, 56,
　62, *64*
　classification frameworks 6
　commonalities and differences 6–7
　defining features of 56
　definition 5
　discrepancy between goals and
　　current status 58–9
　and exploration 56–7
　　similarities with 58
　importance of 56–7
　positive affect 11–12
　positive behaviour 5
　see also behavioural perspective;
　　behavioural system model of
　　proactivity
　proactive discrepancy production
　　59
proactive goals *62*, 63, *64*
proactive person-environment fit
　behaviour 6
proactive personality 3–4
　correlation with attachment style
　　71

proactive strategic behaviour 6
proactivity *see* employee proactivity
proactivity personality 71
process perspective 7–8
process view of personality 87, 89
prototype attachment style 44–5, 46
psychoanalytic paradigm 15
　comparison with attachment theory
　　16–18
psychological contracts 79–80, 81
psychological safety 77

R

reactive discrepancy reduction 59
reason to pathway 8, 9–10, 14
reciprocity 86
reflecting 8
regulatory energy 59, 60, *62*
relational energy 74
relational experiences 13–14, 15
relational psychological contracts
　80–1
relational schemas 51, 53, 54
research 83
　future avenues of study 91–8
　integration of knowledge 91
responsive caregiving 94
Rhoades, L. and Eisenberger, R. 78
Richards, D.A. and Hackett, R.D. 98
romantic attachment style 46
romantic relationships 49–50

S

secondary attachment figures 43
secure attachment 33, 34, 35, 37–8,
　39, 67–9, 70
　balance and autonomy 40–1
　clear and well-organized self-
　　concept 38–9
　expectations of negative outcomes
　　40
　expectations of positive outcomes
　　40
　future-oriented 68
　positive feedback 38
　positive if-then expectancies 40
　positive model of others 39
　response to negative attachment-
　　relevant events 41

secure base 73–5, 79, 96–7
 and leadership 93–4
security-attachment related
 experiences 51–2
security priming 50, 51–3
 studies
  Gillath and Shaver 52, 53
self-concept
 and ambivalent attachment 70
 negative 38–9
 positive 38, 39
self-efficacy 9, 59–60, 68, 74
self-esteem 68
self-initiated proactive behaviour 5
self-initiative 12
self-regulation resources 63, 64
self-views, positive 63–4, 68
servant leadership 76–7
set goals 25, 27, 28, 31
sexual behavioural system 29, 30, 31
Shaver et al. 102
social exchange approach 85–6
 differences from attachment
  approach 85–6
social groups 72
social interaction 72
sociometer theory 63–4, 68
specific relational models 45–6
spreading activation theory of
  memory 50–1
state self-evaluations 92
structure view of personality 87
sub-goals 27
supervisor-specific attachment 46
supervisors 72
 secure-base support 93–4
 support for employees 73, 74
 and transformational leadership
  75–6
support-seeking process 95–6

T

target-specific proactivity 86
task performance 99
traditional psychoanalytic paradigms
  see psychoanalytic paradigm

trait agreeableness 84–5
traits 87, 88
transactional psychological contracts
  80
transformational leadership 75–6
two-level approach to personality
  91–3

V

voice 61
voice behaviour 100

W

within-individual level 91, 92–3
work behaviour 99–103
 classifications of 99–100, 101
 goal-corrected behavioural system
  99, 100–1, 102–3
work engagement 12
work role 10–11
work teams 77–8
 research 98–9
Wu, C.-H. and Parker, S.K. 73, 74,
  75, 92